DUDLEY PUBLIC LIBRARIES

The loan of this book may be renewed if not required by other readers, by contacting the library from which it was borrowed.

28-10-11		
30. NOV 31.12.2015		

▲ This solid-looking brick and wrought-iron entrance stands outside Harwich Town station, at the end of the old Great Eastern Railway branch line from Manningtree in Essex. On 13 February 1982 a Cravens two-car diesel multiple unit (DMU) stands at the platform, while to the right a rake of 'Cartics' stands at the car terminal.

Another freight terminal was located at nearby Parkeston Quay station, renamed Harwich International in 1995. For many years, Harwich has had maritime links with the Hook of Holland, and at times with Esbjerg in Denmark and Antwerp in Belgium, with 'Continental Express' trains connecting with ferries. The 1854 branch line is now marketed as the 'Mayflower Line'. *Author*

▲ Although the origins of the Severn Beach branch date back to the 1860s, with the alignment being modified in the 1870s, it would be 1922 before the current terminus was reached. This diverse and scenic line traverses deep cuttings, viaducts and embankments with perhaps the mile-long Clifton Down Tunnel being the major engineering feature. The frequent service on this Community Rail line is part sponsored by Bristol City Council. With Stapleton Road station in the far background, single power car No B132 passes children at play as it leaves the main line (since 'dequadrified') at Narroways Hill Junction, and takes to the single-line branch on 16 July 1980. *Author*

THE RISE AND FALL OF BRITISH RAILWAYS

BRANCH & MINOR LINES

JOHN VAUGHAN

Haynes Publishing

First published in 2011 by Haynes Publishing

A catalogue record for this book is available from the British Library.

ISBN 978 1 84425 704 1

Library of Congress control no. 2011923586

Published by Haynes Publishing,
Sparkford, Yeovil, Somerset BA22 7JJ, UK

Tel: 01963 442030 Fax: 01963 440001
Int. tel: +44 1963 442030 Int. fax: +44 1963 440001
E-mail: sales@haynes.co.uk
Website: www.haynes.co.uk

Haynes North America Inc., 861 Lawrence Drive,
Newbury Park, California 91320, USA

Printed in the USA by Odcombe Press LP,
1299 Bridgestone Parkway, La Vergne, TN 37086

Recognition

In compiling this volume I have relied on a number of colleagues for the supply of specific photographic material. I thank all of the photographers shown in the caption credits, but worthy of special mention are Michael Mensing, Gavin Morrison, Brian Lewis of the Stephenson Locomotive Society and Brian Morrison, who all took time and trouble to meet special requirements. I would also like to pay tribute to the photographers from the past, who are no longer with us but who recorded the railway scene for future generations to subsequently enjoy, particularly the late W.A. (Cam) Camwell, H.C. (Henry) Casserley, S.C. (Sid) Nash, R.C. (Dick) Riley and Geoffrey Bannister. I would also like to acknowledge the help of Peter Nicholson, Steve Davies, and my very good friends John Hicks and the late and much-missed John Frith, a lifelong branch line enthusiast.

CONTENTS

INTRODUCTION

To THE RAILWAY ENTHUSIAST there is nothing more charming and evocative than a rural branch line. To the railway romantic, branches and minor lines immediately project an image of peace and charm where a twisting single track passes meadows and streams in perhaps a shallow valley, with the gentle pace of a small train comprising a coach or two, interrupted only by a brief pause at a small country station or a wayside halt. Perhaps a local inhabitant might catch one of the infrequent trains or a parcel, package or mail bag might be deposited on the platform requiring the attention of the railwayman who is likely to be performing several roles. At slightly larger stations there might be a passing loop and even a signalbox where single-line tokens are exchanged or a semaphore signal or two pulled off, giving confidence to the few passengers that it is safe to proceed. Passengers are likely to know the train crew and station staff by name and there would be time for a chat, with the weather being the favourite subject.

There would normally be a station approach road and perhaps a red telephone box to greet passengers. The size or even grandeur of the branch terminus station would in many cases not be commensurate with the volume of railway traffic, and to that extent be over-built, possibly with accommodation provided for the stationmaster or railway staff. Inside the front door there would be a ticket office with often just a small ticket window facing would-be travellers. Posters would advertise popular destinations for holidays by rail and special events, such as market days. At stations rather than halts there would be a waiting room and occasionally waiting rooms that sometimes divided either the sexes or the passengers' chosen class of travel. In winter, a roaring fire would normally be provided with the coal being retrieved from the pile beside the signalbox, which had been delivered by the local pick-up goods.

The goods train would often work once per day setting down and picking up a handful of wagons as it went about its business at a leisurely pace with only the crashing of buffers, the clanking of coupling chains or the squeal of wheel flanges to disturb the peace. There might be seasonal peaks and troughs of activity as perhaps sugar beet or livestock were loaded. Above all else, coal would be delivered and a local merchant would often operate out of the goods yard. All traffic would be wagonload with not a block train in sight.

With the infrequency of trains there would often be quieter moments where station staff or signalmen tended platform flowerbeds, hedgerows or even small vegetable patches. The station would be free of litter and white lines on the platform edges would be pristine. Fire buckets would be full of water and other important facilities attended to. Depending on the era, the platform lamps would be illuminated by oil and wick, gas and mantle, or electricity and bulb, although it is worth pointing out that both oil and gas survived in a handful of locations until the late 20th century. Quite often the village station would be a social centre with perhaps a 'Railway Inn' nearby and in many locations the daily newspapers for the area would be carried by the first inbound train of the day with the post leaving on the last outbound train of the day. Some branch and minor lines were quite eccentric in their mode of operation, while others that were built on wildly optimistic forecasts of likely traffic, were so little used that they were abandoned long before the words 'closure' and 'Beeching' became part of the common vocabulary.

In architectural terms there was a wide range of station buildings at the terminus of many branches. Most were built at 90° to the running lines, parallel to the stop blocks, while others faced the running lines. The size and grandeur of the buildings reflected the original building capital and the financial strength of the railway company. Some light railways made great use of wood and corrugated iron whereas the affluent major railway companies provided buildings that appeared to be more of a status symbol than a practical place of business. Often, a small engine shed would be provided to accommodate the branch locomotive and as often as not there would be a goods shed, the provision of a crane being a practical bonus.

Larger stations had goods docks and cattle pens and an early benefit was the provision of a telegraph office at some locations. On the opening of the branch line the local price of coal was often halved and the railways facilitated the adoption of the standard Greenwich Mean Time across the land. Larger rural stations provided much employment with a complete hierarchy of staff in post. This might include stationmaster, his clerk, booking office clerk, goods clerk, signalman, porter, driver, fireman, guard, nearby crossing keepers, platelayers and gangers, with some activities requiring more than a single shift. Branches and minor lines often helped the development of an area even though the railway operation itself was loss-making.

Most branch and minor lines were built before the advent of motorised transport and particularly the arrival of the motor bus. The arrival of the railway enabled the local population to travel and although initially this would be the privilege of the upper and middle classes some provision was made for poorer souls with such innovations as the cheap 'parliamentary ticket', normally available on the first train of the day. Just as the railways had substantially replaced the horse-drawn coach and the commercial canals, branch and minor lines were also to experience significant competition in the Edwardian era, now a century ago, from the far more flexible motor omnibus.

One of the great problems with many branch lines was that they were built 'on the cheap', which meant that the permanent way followed the easiest contours. As a result many hill towns and villages or even those on the 'wrong' side of a valley or river could be up to two miles away from the station that carried the town's name. As competition hotted up fares came under pressure and in some areas buses offered a better frequency of service than the train, so much so that many railway companies became bus operators, particularly the Great Western Railway. On the freight side the motor lorry also began to attack what had almost been a railway monopoly, thereby eroding a percentage of the goods traffic takings. The railways fought back by starting local delivery services using their own vehicles, operating from their various goods yards.

Suddenly there was more of a focus on costs with perhaps greater awareness of a profit-and-loss account with the shareholders in mind. The optimum railway network in terms of route miles was achieved just before the First World War with a total of 23,440 route miles being recorded. Although a handful of branches and minor lines were built after the First World War the combination of the great depression in the late 1920s and early 1930s, and road competition, did nothing to help branch line receipts, as amounts of disposable income dwindled. The motor bus was becoming more sophisticated with increases in speed, comfort, flexibility and reliability. By contrast the trains on many branches comprised an elderly locomotive that had been decanted and 'put out to grass', coupled to rolling stock that comprised redundant main line vehicles, which became increasingly shabby. There were significant branch line closures between 1920 and 1939 and few realise that during this period, 1,264 route miles of railway line were closed. In the main, these closures concerned lines that were hopelessly unremunerative with little prospect of encouraging traffic in sufficient volumes to turn them around financially. Indeed, many independent lines spent decades in receivership and were effectively bankrupt.

What was emerging was the stark realisation that the romantic branch line image so beloved amongst railway enthusiasts was at the opposite end of the spectrum from the nuts and bolts of high finance, where somebody somewhere had to underwrite the sometimes considerable losses incurred by the fully staffed, fully signalled branch line. The sight of a dedicated locomotive with its single coach containing perhaps half a dozen passengers trundling through the countryside came at a considerable price.

The Second World War had a negative impact on branch and minor lines in that there had been no inward investment in such routes and they groaned along with an infrastructure that was often a delight to railway enthusiasts, but which was not conducive to trouble-free operation or in projecting a slick, modern and proactive public transport system. Many of the problems were both serious and nationwide in nature and the post-war Labour Government decided to nationalise the entire British UK mainland railway network (and other transportation systems). These railway assets had mainly been owned since the 1923 Grouping by the 'Big Four' railway companies, although it is often overlooked that 55 other railway undertakings were also absorbed into British Railways (BR) upon nationalisation in 1948. BR was the trading name of the Railway Executive, which in turn was an organisation with certain delegated authorities under the auspices of the British Transport Commission (BTC). The BTC was inaugurated on 1 January 1948 under the chairmanship of Lord Hurcombe. The organisation was unwieldy, with 688,000 employees across all transport disciplines!

Within a year, a Branch Line Committee was appointed with a remit to identify and close the least-used and therefore greatest loss-making branch lines. As a result of their deliberations a considerable number of minor routes were closed in the late 1940s and early to mid-1950s. In fact, even while the 1955 Modernisation Plan was being

► Rightly or wrongly, the late Dr Richard Beeching, later Lord Beeching (1913–85), the first Chairman of the British Railways Board (successor to the British Transport Commission), will always be associated with branch and minor line closures. All over the UK new housing estates have been built on land once owned by the railway, resulting in numerous Beeching Ways, Beeching Drives and Beeching Closes, such is the English sense of humour. This example was photographed at the site of Halwill Junction station in Devon. *Author*

◄ This remarkably rare photograph shows railbus No 29952, one of three vehicles manufactured by Leyland Motors Ltd in 1933. They were powered by a small 130hp Leyland engine, weighed just 13 tons and conveyed 40 passengers. The diminutive unit is seen at Coalburn in Scotland on 8 June 1949 with the 11.12am to Hamilton, shortly before its withdrawal. *W.A. Camwell/SLS*

drafted, closures continued apace, long before the arrival of Dr Richard Beeching. Few realise that between 1948 and 1962 a whopping 3,318 miles of railway line closed, much of it in the branch and minor line category. Financially, the railways more or less held their own until 1952, due mainly to a lack of capital expenditure. But the railways were worn out and during the next decade, prior to the Beeching years, losses accumulated at an alarming rate, especially as the Modernisation Plan had effectively authorised hundreds of millions of pounds of expenditure at today's values.

By 1962, the railways were losing a staggering £104 million (over £1.6 billion at 2011 values) and clearly something had to be done. Although explained in more detail in a later chapter, in 1963 'The Reshaping of British Railways' report was published and this document exposed some startling facts, facts that would be disputed for decades to come. It transpired that 30 per cent of BR track miles carried only 1 per cent of passengers and only 1 per cent of freight, and that half of the total stations on the network together contributed just 2 per cent of income. Even a railway optimist could not argue that these results would and perhaps should have resulted in considerable rationalisation. If they had all been adopted the report's recommendations would have reduced the network from 18,000 to just 12,000 route miles.

The implementation of the report was to impose the death sentence on a huge number of lesser-used lines and stations and the expression 'Beeching cuts' became a household word. From 1963 branch lines closed on an almost weekly basis and in the main those availing themselves of the objections process found their various appeals falling on stony ground, especially as statistics showed that most of the lines scheduled for closure had local bus services available, which effectively duplicated the train service. The first hint of recognition that railways performed a social service emerged with the 1968 Transport Act, but closures continued into

the mid-1970s when by and large, they ceased as political pressure from the public in marginal constituencies, where services were threatened, became more acute. Also, slowly but surely, green credentials and environmental issues became fashionable, virtually halting closures, although by then the damage was substantially done.

Since then there has, encouragingly, been some regeneration of branch and minor lines. Indeed, some lines have been reopened and scores of new stations have appeared. Some branch lines have been electrified and there has been considerable inward investment. Under sectorisation and later privatisation there has not only been consolidation but some plans have been tabled to completely reinstate closed railway lines for passenger services. Although in the present financial climate these ideas may be little more than pipe dreams it seems that there may, after all, be a future for the time-honoured British branch line.

At a personal level I have a lifetime of memories of travel and photography on innumerable branch and minor lines, many of them now long closed. I have been interested in branch lines for over 50 years and I have had the pleasure, indeed privilege, of writing about them over many decades. Several of my visits were with my late and much-missed friend John Frith and I dedicate this book to his memory. In completing this substantial task I have been assisted by photographic contributions from a number of colleagues and organisations and they are mentioned in the Recognition section. It has been a pleasure compiling this tome for Haynes Publishing and it is my sincere wish that you, the reader, experience equal enjoyment and plenty of nostalgia in palming the pages.

John Vaughan
Goring by Sea
June 2011

GROUPING AND FORMATION

IN ORDER TO SET THE SCENE that resulted in the introduction of branch railway lines in the UK, it is worth spending some time briefly summarising general background history regarding the development of railways and transportation generally. It would be from the foundation stones of the early years that the railways and consequently the branches would be built, assisted by commercial aspirations and entrepreneurs, combined with growing technology.

Railways or at least wagonways can be traced back to 600BC when boats were transported across the Isthmus of Corinth on the Diolkos Wagonway. Early tramways used grooves cut in limestone as guides, the predecessor of rails. There is evidence of wagonways in Europe from about 1350 and wooden rails were demonstrably in use by 1515. Industrial wagonway use in Germany was commonplace in the 16th century and ore tubs on rails were illustrated from 1556. In the United Kingdom, wooden rails were used at industrial sites in Shropshire from 1605 and by the 18th century the use of wooden rails between coal mines and staithes (shipping points) were commonplace in the Newcastle upon Tyne region. Other areas where early wagonways were in use included South Wales and Cornwall, and in industrial environments around pits, mines and quarries. By 1750, L-shaped metal plates were joined up to form plateways and by 1810 this form of track was widely used in South Wales and also, for example, on the Poldice (or Portreath) Tramway in Cornwall.

Proper railways using metal tracks that were secured in either metal or granite chairs or setts soon followed. Most of these early railways comprised cast-iron rails and wagons were either man or horse powered and, where fitted, crude braking systems were employed. On inclines, ropes and later cables were used to lift and lower wagons, power being provided by horses and capstans, stationary steam engines, or in a few cases, waterwheels. Descending wagons were balanced by ascending loads on some inclines. At the same time, early forms of locomotion were being developed and the first full-size steam locomotive to appear was in 1804 and is credited to the Cornishman Richard Trevithick.

Arising from an Act for a horse-powered plateway, placed before Parliament in 1821, the Stockton & Darlington Railway opened in 1825. This was claimed to be the world's first public railway opened for freight and passengers, although the latter was something of an afterthought. The 26-mile line ran from Stockton to Darlington, later continuing to various coal mines in the Shildon area. The line employed the steam locomotives *Locomotion* and later *Experiment,* the former engine being credited with hauling the first ever passenger train, albeit taking two hours to travel 12 miles. In the early days both locomotives and horses were used to power loads. The line was extended to Middlesbrough in 1833 and from that time all movements were locomotive hauled. In the meantime, the Liverpool & Manchester Railway was being built and what is generally acknowledged as the first modern public railway opened in 1830, although simultaneous developments were occurring in other countries.

In 1829, prior to opening, the famous Rainhill Trials were conducted where such pioneers as *Novelty, Cyclops, Perseverance, Rocket* and *Sans Pareil* were all put through their paces. As every schoolboy knows, Stephenson's *Rocket* was the winner. Liverpool was already a major port and Manchester was a large, well-established manufacturing centre with both cities having substantial populations and so the proposed link had the best possible chance of succeeding. Forecasts were made regarding the volumes of merchandise that could be moved by rail, the charges that could be levied, the costs of operation and the likely profit that the shareholders might enjoy. Similar assessments had been conducted by the earlier canal builders and similar calculations would be used in the forthcoming decades when, predictably, the majority of the larger British ports were to become rail connected.

Even at minor ports and harbours the commercial activity was measured in terms of incoming and outbound tonnage, and was used in calculations to test the financial viability of constructing a railway line or branch. Many small harbours were also to be served by rail, for example Portreath in Cornwall in 1812, Canterbury to Whitstable in Kent from 1830, and Newquay in 1849. In terms of seafaring in the now far-off days of sail, early tradesmen transported goods over unbelievably long distances, in some instances spanning continents. Small vessels of the schooner variety generally carried a payload of up to 200 tons and travelled shorter distances, very much akin to the role of the 'coaster'. They serviced a wide range of mainly smaller ports and harbours where it was necessary for ships to have only a shallow draught. (The draught of a ship is measured as the vertical distance from the waterline to the bottom of the hull or keel. Draught therefore determines the minimum depth of water required for a ship or boat to safely navigate. Generally speaking, the heavier and larger the ship the greater the draught and therefore the deeper the water in a port or harbour needs to be.)

◄ The rural delights of the British branch line are shown in this June 1934 view of the Looe branch in Cornwall. The line on the right towards the stop blocks served the remote Coombe Junction station (behind the photographer) where, since 1901, Liskeard to Looe branch trains have reversed direction. The line in the foreground is part of the run-round loop for branch passenger train locomotives and that on the left is the freight line to the Moorswater works of English China Clays (originally continuing to the quarries and mines around Caradon Hill). In the background the main line is carried 150ft above the valley floor on Moorswater Viaduct. Although included in the original Beeching Reshaping Report 'hit list' the Looe Valley line is still open and now the occasional cement train runs down to Moorswater, the site of the old china clay driers. *Author's collection*

◄ This wonderful group portrait of the Looe station staff was taken in 1911 and is typical of the manpower then employed at fairly modest branch line termini. At today's values the annual wage bill for this group would have been about £0.25 million. The positions or grades held by the staff can easily be deduced with perhaps the stationmaster, engine driver and guard being the most obvious. Six of the group are sporting GWR hats. In the background is No 13, a GWR 4-4-0 saddle tank built in 1886, which was resident on the line from 1902 until 1922. Except for the train crew the branch has been unmanned since 1981, when Coombe Junction signalbox closed. *Author's collection*

For longer distances, including voyages from the UK to Canada and the Far East, much larger, fully rigged ships of the era with a cargo capacity of up to 500 tons were used and these vessels required deep-water harbours. Gradually, the design of ships improved, even heavier payloads were carried and the size and speed of ships increased. By the time metal-hulled but wind-powered windjammers were built in the late Victorian era, the payload had grown tenfold and with the arrival of steamships this increased further. Many of the smaller ports that could not accommodate these larger vessels became redundant, being reduced to small-scale fishing activities.

Since the beginning of time, overland transportation had relied on mules and horses fitted with suitable panniers for the movement of goods of every description. The Romans had recognised the need for a road network, but for centuries, long after their departure, cross-country travel was via crude tracks. A horse-drawn dray or sledge was sometimes used but in the late 18th century simple wagons (as distinct from the previously mentioned tubs) started to appear. Members of the aristocracy began to use coaches for travel around their estates. It was clear that the primitive pothole-ridden tracks with crude bridges at river crossings and a virtual absence of infrastructure, such as drainage systems, needed to be improved, leading to a national network of roads. Such improvements would obviously cost large sums of money and consequently Turnpike Trusts were created. These Trusts were effectively businesses whereby tracks were improved, widened and graded with the cost being recovered from road users by means of toll charges, which were collected at strategically placed toll gates or houses. The early turnpikes were virtually unusable in winter as wagons made deep ruts in the primitive surface.

By the early 19th century, road surfaces had improved so much that stage coaches were in use, enabling the affluent members of the community to travel more freely from town to town but at a price. With the coming of the Industrial Revolution from the middle of the 18th century, road-going freight wagons with a tare of about 3 tons were in use. These would be hauled by between three and six horses, depending on the terrain. Eventually, a network of coach routes and roads covered the length and breadth of the country but they were no match for railway lines in the mass transportation of the population, raw materials and manufactured goods. The stage coach era in the UK was relatively short-lived due to the coming of the railways and in particular, from the start of the 20th century, the arrival of the motor bus, and in our cities, the street tram. In some remote parts of the country horse-drawn coaches continued performing the function of omnibuses until the First World War. Surprisingly, horse power on our railways continued until the 1960s, for example shunting wagons at Hayle Wharves in Cornwall and at Newmarket in Cambridgeshire. Just as the railways largely eliminated canal usage and horse-drawn transport it was the automobile, omnibus and motor lorry that would substantially damage the railways, in terms of the carriage of both freight and passenger traffic.

Returning to the Liverpool and Manchester area, it seems strange that one of the last great UK canals to be completed in 1894 was the Manchester Ship Canal, despite the existence of the Liverpool & Manchester Railway. In setting the branch and minor line scene the history of canals, like the roads and shipping, should be briefly mentioned. It is necessary to travel back in time to the 10th century when the Grand Canal of China was in operation. However, there can be problems in identifying a true canal. Many of the earliest schemes could be called 'river improvements' that facilitated not only transport but also drainage. A UK example would be the Fossdyke that was built by the Romans in about AD50 between Lincoln and the River Trent. Early European examples of canal building include the 1398-built Stecknitz Canal, between Luebeck and the Elbe, and the 150-mile-long Canal du Midi in France, which was completed in 1681.

Several early projects in the UK were so-called 'river navigations', which were effectively short detours away from river courses to aid navigation by small craft. One such example was the 1563-built Exeter Canal, which avoided part of the River Exe, allowing craft to reach the city. Similarly before eventually becoming the St Helens Canal, purpose-built channels helped in the navigation of Sankey Brook between St Helens and Liverpool. In the middle of the 18th century a number of canal projects were instigated as a result of the urgent need to transport goods in bulk to feed the Industrial Revolution, which was rapidly gaining momentum. Although not for this tome the sociological and demographic changes at this time were enormous and the potential benefits of canals became well established.

Although there were significant projects being undertaken nationwide, focussed mainly on industrial areas, it was the Bridgewater Canal that is generally recognised as being the first purpose-built commercial canal in the UK. Under the direction of the Duke of Bridgewater a six-mile canal was built between Manchester and coal mines in the Worsley area. The engineer James Brindley made sure that the canal was in full operation by 1776. After this date canals were opened thick and fast but with no nationwide standards and so canals built on a budget were normally narrower than the main waterways. There was a slowdown during an economic depression in the early 1780s, but just as there was to be a period of 'railwaymania' there was a period of 'canalmania' when some quite marginal schemes were approved, including 'branch' canals. By 1840 there were 4,500 miles of canals in operation within the UK with a single horse often pulling a 40-ton barge, compared with three horses pulling 3-tons on the roads and turnpikes. Canals were slow but efficient and in some areas the opening of a canal would halve the price of coal for village and city dwellers.

However, from the middle of the 19th century, railways began to seriously impact the viability of canals and during the next 100 years canal closures were a regular feature of the national transport scene. In some cases railway companies purchased canal companies outright in order to eliminate any opposition. Such canals experienced a rapid decline as routine maintenance was withdrawn. Horse-drawn barges eventually gave way to motorised craft as the internal combustion engine was developed, but that in itself was insufficient to reverse the terminal decline in traffic. Although a modicum of freight is still conveyed by canal the talk since the 1950s has been more about canal restoration and the leisure industry than commercial activity.

At the time of opening of the Liverpool & Manchester Railway other main lines were in the various stages of planning and within a few years future main lines were being opened on an almost monthly basis. These lines were to connect all major centres of population. For example, the Grand Junction Railway from Liverpool to Birmingham opened in 1837, which linked with the London & Birmingham Railway the following year. By the early 1840s main trunk routes were being constructed, extended and joined on a frequent basis as a national network was steadily being formed. In 1845 there were 650 Railway Acts passed by Parliament authorising the construction of 9,000 route miles of track. It is estimated that over 200,000 navvies were employed on railway construction nationwide. However, at about this time the railway building bubble, popularly known as 'railwaymania', burst following a credit squeeze, subsequent financial crisis, rising prices and inflation. Building works on many main lines slowed considerably and in some cases stopped altogether as the clouds of recession gathered. It would be several years before many projects would be completed as money was hard to come by well into the mid-1850s.

As early as 1839, Bradshaw had produced his first timetable and by 1841 this evolved into *Bradshaw's Monthly Railway Guide*. The original eight-page product had expanded to 32 pages by 1845 and by 1896, long after Bradshaw's death, the tome reached a remarkable 946 pages. This increase in size was broadly commensurate with the extraordinary growth in the railway network. With the exception of lines such as the Great Central Railway route into the Capital, it would be reasonable to say that most primary routes were largely in place by 1860. As regards branch and minor lines, once the main trunk routes were established branch lines grew, as in the branches of a tree, to serve towns and major villages that were not directly served by the main lines. However, there were many notable exceptions where railways were built in complete isolation of the main routes or the major companies. A good example of such a line is the Bodmin & Wadebridge Railway, which was the first line in Cornwall to employ standard gauge steam locomotives to haul passenger trains. This line opened as early as 1834 and was not connected by rail to the 'outside world' until 1888, and to its parent company in 1895!

The benefits of having a railway to serve a centre of population or a large industrial site were obvious for all to see, especially the well-informed members of the gentry and the higher echelons of society who had investment and profits in mind. In the right circumstances there was money to be made out of the railway age as economic equations were tested, comparing forecast building and other capital costs versus the estimated income from both freight and passenger sources. Landowners, members of the business community and merchants all had a vested interest in ensuring that their particular town was rail served. There was normally a primary mover of a motion to build a line, quite often a titled member of the aristocracy, and a public meeting would be held. An engineer would be employed to conduct initial surveys, plan a favourable route, perform various quantity surveying activities, and provide an estimate of construction and other costs. Based on the length of line, the local topography and the customer's specification the engineer would calculate the amount of money that needed to be raised. The primary purpose of the meeting would be to seek assurances of financial support from would-be shareholders.

All proposals for new railway lines required an Act of Parliament, and a fortune was made by legal representatives who were employed to process the plans through the various legal requirement stages. A prospectus was normally issued and this would contain information regarding the proposition as a whole, the various markets and businesses to be served, likely traffic projections and financial forecasts. Flexibility was often a factor when the proposers would promise to provide private sidings to serve individual farms and businesses. It is not surprising to relate that all of these financial cases contained exaggerated traffic figures and therefore inflated potential income yield. Social benefits were wildly optimistic because the poorer classes were unlikely to have the time or wherewithal to use the railway but the population at large would gain from cheaper coal and other essential commodities. The costs associated with the railway were always understated, but overall the glowing terminology was often sufficient to persuade ditherers that they would be making a wise and profitable investment in buying railway company shares. Often, approval was given for construction of the line and the raising of funds with authority to raise further capital if necessary. In other cases railway companies ran out of capital and had to return to Parliament to seek approval to raise further funds.

Even if an Act of Parliament was passed the working capital still had to be raised and often early promises of funding did not result in the purchase of shares. Many notable members of the aristocracy wanted a railway built, but not on their immediate doorstep, choosing to influence the route of the line. Others made special stipulations such as having a private station located on their estate for personal use. In other instances the gentry

▲ The little three-mile three-chains branch line from Fort Brockhurst on the Fareham to Gosport line in Hampshire, down to Lee-on-the-Solent, opened in May 1894. Work had started in 1891 but was delayed due to a defaulting contractor. Three intermediate halts were opened at a later date to maximise takings. There were no signals and operations were under the 'one engine in steam' principle. One of the early locomotives used on the line was No 21 *Scott*, which was built by George England in 1862 and named after the General Manager of the LSWR. It was purchased from the Somerset & Dorset Railway in 1871 and rebuilt in 1887. The quaint train is seen in the bay platform at Fort Brockhurst in 1900. The line closed to passengers from 1 January 1931 and to freight on 2 October 1935. *Author's collection*

▼ This view shows the classic scene where a single-track branch line, normally ending in a branch bay platform, connects with a main line station, this time at Churston in south Devon. This Brixham-bound branch train has a luggage wagon and three ancient coaches in tow, including a clerestory example. On the right is the Paignton to Kingswear line and in the background is the rather austere-looking Railway Hotel. Purely by chance, the locomotive featured is, again, No 13 an 1886 GWR 4-4-0 saddle tank (see page 10). Being resident on the Looe branch from 1902 until 1922 and scrapped in 1926 the photograph is probably Victorian. The Brixham branch closed in May 1963 while the 'main' line is now preserved and operated as the Dartmouth Steam Railway. *Author's collection*

Churston Station & Hotel

wanted the railway 'hidden' in a tunnel or deep cutting. There were sometimes objections to railway practices, a regular complaint being construction work taking place on the Sabbath. It was not unusual for the contractor to 'go bust' and for new contractors to be employed, resulting in construction delays. Some of these contractors were inexperienced in railway building and some were just plain incompetent. Little regard was had to health and safety matters and there were some horrendous accidents during construction, including many fatalities. The navvies were often rowdy and they soon gained a bad reputation in local communities. The most frequent complaint was drunkenness as chunks of the weekly wage were squandered on alcohol on pay days.

Once construction had been completed the line could not be opened until a rigorous inspection by the Board of Trade. The inspectors were often qualified ex-military men who examined all aspects of safety and construction standards throughout. They were normally provided with a special inspection train and often there had to be some remedial work and a re-inspection before the line could open. No two lines were alike as some were built economically on a modest budget while others were extravagant in terms of buildings and the quality of engineering. Some lines had grand and stylish stations, artistic embellishments, a quality permanent way and full signalling, with copious sidings, while others used lighter rail, wooden frames and corrugated iron in the construction of the major buildings with a minimalist approach. Once approved grand opening days would be planned and these always involved the local population. There would be bunting in the streets, a decorated train, a procession including civil dignitaries, local associations and the mandatory brass band. There would be long and positive speeches about the great future the railway would offer the town and how everybody would become more prosperous.

Buns were given to children, beer to the workers, with the VIPs normally enjoying a multi-course meal at a superior hotel, where more speeches would be made.

The days following the opening inevitably produced a note of reality as the few branch trains (normally between two and six round trips per day) trundled backwards and forwards with just a sprinkling of passengers. A cameo of a country branch line and a country station is given in the Introduction and will not be repeated here, suffice to say that elements of over-manning and the over-provision of facilities on some lines were not uncommon. Many branches and minor lines offered first-, second- and third-class accommodation and fares, in addition to the mandatory 'parliamentary tickets', even though less than 10 per cent of income came from the premier class of passenger. After a couple of years of operation many branch lines were in financial difficulty and their only option was to persuade the nearest main line company to take over the operation of their line or to come to a leasing arrangement. A classic example was the Cornish Minerals Railway that opened for goods in 1874 and to passengers in 1876 but by 1877 a deal was made with the Great Western Railway to operate the lines, which they acquired outright in 1896.

Acquisitions normally resulted in the operating company retaining large percentages of the 'take' with the directors and shareholders of the original local company often receiving a fraction of their original investment. A few branches came to Schemes of Arrangement with their creditors and kept running even though technically bankrupt. Some lines, such as the Bishop's Castle Railway in Shropshire, continued to operate for decades while in receivership. The most successful lines had a lucrative freight business as well as a solid passenger base, but in sparsely populated rural areas where agriculture was the primary business activity times were often hard.

◀ Another ancient train in Victorian times, accompanied by posing railway staff, plus one paper boy delivering the *Daily Mercury*, is seen at the single platform at Praze station on the Helston branch line in Cornwall. Plans to link Helston with Hayle by plateway date back to 1819 but the line was never built and it would not be until May 1887 that a branch opened between Gwinear Road on the GWR main line and Helston. Despite summer holiday traffic and loads of seasonal broccoli the line was a loss-maker and it closed to passengers in November 1962 and to freight in October 1964. A short section of track has been relaid at Trevarno with a view to long-term preservation of part of the branch. *Author's collection*

▲ The history of the branch line between Moreton-in-Marsh and Shipston-on-Stour had its origins in a standard gauge horse-drawn tramway between Stratford-upon-Avon and Moreton, dating back to 1836. It was 1889 before legislation was passed enabling the (by then) GWR to operate steam-hauled trains on the branch. In the meantime, the old tramway north of Shipston had ceased to operate in early Edwardian times and the track was lifted in 1918, the year the route was officially abandoned. Traffic was meagre and the branch closed to passengers as early as July 1929 and to freight in May 1960. In this vintage view the intermediate station of Stretton-on-Fosse is shown. Opened in 1892 there is plenty to note including two running-in boards on the short platform, prefabricated buildings, milk churns, single goods wagon in the single siding, railwayman, offspring and dog, plus assorted handcarts. *Author's collection*

▼ Another wonderful animated branch line terminus view featuring the old wooden station building of Gilfach in Glamorganshire, 184 miles from London, Paddington. This is yet another example of an early line closure, demonstrating that there were scores of branch line casualties long before the 1960s 'Beeching era'. The line from Blackmill briefly closed and reopened in March 1928, only to finally close to passengers in September 1930, a victim of the great depression. In 1910, there were just four trains per day Monday to Friday with a couple of extras on Saturday, the 4¾-mile journey taking 15 minutes. *Author's collection*

By 1880, most small towns that were not served by a main line were connected thereto by a branch or cross-country line. To facilitate the construction of lines to smaller towns and villages a Light Railways Act was passed in 1896. Under the Act railway lines of lighter construction, sufficient to take an 8-ton axle load but with a 25mph speed limit, were permitted. There was also a reduction in paper work and 'red tape' saving both time and money. Early examples of lines built under such legislation were the Kent & East Sussex Railway, the Kelvedon & Tollesbury Light Railway and the narrow-gauge Leek & Manifold Valley Light Railway. By 1910, just before the railways of the UK were at their zenith in network route mileage, even important hamlets were served by rail, a situation helped by the introduction of 'halts' during the Edwardian era. In many areas, especially along industrial valleys, there were often rival but duplicate routes. However, for many minor lines the clouds were gathering as the motor bus arrived with a vengeance. Buses operated from the town or village centre and bus stops were plentiful and routes flexible enough to serve lucrative pick-up points.

The advent of the First World War did not help matters and indeed, branch services were suspended on some lines. On a handful of lines the tracks were actually lifted for the war effort, such as the Basingstoke & Alton Light Railway. The subject of the railways in wartime is dealt with in the next chapter. Some branch and minor lines did not fully recover and the 1923 Grouping of railway companies into the so-called 'Big Four' did not help the fate of many rural but unquestionably loss-making lines. There were years of industrial disputes involving miners and railwaymen culminating in a general strike. By the end of the 1920s the great depression had arrived, leading to a very significant number of railway closures between 1929 and 1935. Financially, even the large companies were struggling and dividends to shareholders all but disappeared. Legal obligations as a 'common carrier' were a financial liability for the railway companies and increased costs unnecessarily. In 1935, Colonel Stephens's Selsey Tramway in West Sussex succumbed to bus competition, being closed by the Southern Railway in 1935. There were scores of other examples.

▼ The Culm Valley branch line from Tiverton Junction to Hemyock was a truly rural line that was supported by local business people and farmers, but which only came to fruition with the financial and operational help of the adjacent main line company. Finally opened in 1876, the line was built on a budget resulting in a permanent way that broadly paralleled the local river, resulting in many tight curves and therefore slow speeds. The radius of these curves necessitated the use of a pair of short, ex-Barry Railway coaches well into BR days. The attractive little station at Hemyock is seen here in about 1912. Note the Lipton's Tea and Pears' Soap adverts on the right, and the cattle dock on the left. The background shed was demolished in 1932. Closure to passengers occurred in September 1963, general freight two years later and milk traffic in October 1975. *Author's collection*

▲ Rural branch line stations came in all shapes and sizes. Some were grand affairs with a full range of offices and permanent accommodation for railway staff while others comprised little more than wooden sheds with corrugated-iron roofs. This fine example was at Langholm in Dumfriesshire, which consisted of a stone building and an all-over roof. The seven-mile branch opened in 1864 and had the distinction of crossing the England/Scotland border. The town prospered on textiles but gradually most of the mills closed. The population was 3,500 in 1901 and 2,300 in 2001! This former North British Railway branch line finally closed to passengers in June 1964 and to freight in September 1967. *SLS*

In the 1951 edition of H.C. Casserley's book *Services Suspended*, over 150 lines are shown as having closed during this period. On many routes attempts to operate on a more economic basis were made including the introduction of various internal combustion-engined vehicles ranging from Ford and Shefflex railcars on some of the Colonel Stephens lines, to the 38 diesel railcars introduced by the Great Western Railway from 1934. The Government provided the 'Big Four' railway companies with loan facilities in 1935, at attractive rates to encourage modernisation via a Railway Finance Corporation, and this resulted in the electrification of some branch lines, mainly on the Southern Railway. Until the advent of the Second World War in 1939, closures continued but at a slower rate. Such lines as Bishop Auckland to Spennymoor, Halifax to

Stainland, the Methven branch in Scotland, the Spilsby branch in Lincolnshire, Uttoxeter to Stafford, the Cleobury Mortimer & Ditton Priors Light Railway, Woodham Ferrers to Maldon East in Essex, and the Devil's Dyke branch near Brighton all closed to passengers, and some completely. During the war years there were restrictions on travel and on some branch lines services were suspended from time to time; for example, the Lostwithiel to Fowey line in Cornwall. However, there were few line closures (see next chapter). Little maintenance was carried out and slowly but surely the infrastructure and equipment became very tired as a 'make-do-and-mend' policy was adopted to save valuable resources. The great days of the 'Big Four' were nearing the end of what would turn out to be a 25-year post-Grouping era.

▲ Just as station buildings came in all shapes and sizes, the same could be said of railway platforms. In addition to stations and halts a variety of platforms were constructed on certain lines to serve hospitals, rifle ranges, golf clubs and industrial works. This example shows the diminutive Silloth Sanatorium Halt in Cumberland (now Cumbria) in 1929. The sanatorium was located just out of frame to the left of this view. Opened in 1856 the Silloth branch served not only the passenger terminus but also extensive dock sidings. Despite the introduction of diesel units from 1954, the branch closed in September 1964, both steam and diesel traction working the strengthened last-day trains. The police attended the departure of the last train from Silloth as thousands of protesters turned up to both commemorate the last train and to vent their anger at the closure. *LGRP/SLS*

▼ The National Rifle Association was formed in 1859 and it was to receive its Royal Charter to facilitate the defence of the realm as a volunteer organisation. The NRA moved from Wimbledon to a 3,000-acre site at Bisley in 1890 and a 1¼-mile branch, then called a 'spur', was constructed between Bisley Camp, seen here, and Brookwood on the LSWR main line. Shooting competitions have been organised for many years and in the First World War, the site was used for military training; witness the military personnel in this photograph of the terminus at that time. The line closed in 1952. *Author's collection*

▲ Her Most Gracious Majesty Queen Victoria laid the foundation stone for a vast, 109-acre military hospital at Netley in 1856, but it was 1863 before the 1,000-bed hospital opened. It was particularly busy during the Boer War and a ¾-mile branch line from Netley station, on the 1866 Portsmouth to Southampton line, to a dedicated platform adjacent to the hospital, was opened in April 1900. Over 50,000 troops were treated in the First World War and 68,000 in the Second World War, many of them disembarking from ships at nearby Southampton. Gradually, the hospital fell into disuse and although rarely used the line did not officially close until December 1963. The vast buildings were demolished in 1966 and today, the site is the Royal Victoria Country Park. Here, a Red Cross train at Netley Hospital station delivers wounded soldiers for medical treatment in about 1915. *Author's collection*

▼ In times gone by footplate crews often had a specific locomotive allocated to them and they would take pride in their machine by keeping the paintwork in pristine condition. This could have been the case at Morthoe in the late 1920s, or Southern Railway (SR) M7 class 0-4-4T No 30 (later No 30030) may have been ex-works. The delightful two-coach branch train from Ilfracombe to Barnstaple Junction is seen entering the station, which was near to the summit of the line. The entire line closed in October 1970 while under the control of the Western Region (WR) of BR. An industrial estate has been built on the site of Ilfracombe station, a common fate. *Author's collection*

▲ In addition to standard-gauge branch lines there were a number of narrow-gauge lines that operated a regular passenger service. Many of these were located in Wales but a famous West Country line was the Lynton & Barnstaple Railway. The 1ft 11½in-gauge line opened in May 1898 and was just over 19 miles long. It connected Barnstaple on the River Taw with Lynton on the north Devon coast. The line ran through sparsely populated countryside and for much of its life was a loss-maker. Having been taken over by the SR at the 1923 Grouping the line was closed in September 1935. This 1938 view shows the remains of Snapper Halt with an old abandoned coach body at the low platform. *Author's collection*

▼ The short Easingwold Railway was a privately owned standard-gauge railway that ran the 2½ miles from Easingwold to Alne station on the East Coast Main Line (ECML). After the original contractor failed, replacement builders completed the line in July 1891 at a cost of £17,000. The branch was profitable until the great depression and again during the Second World War but with a subsequent collapse of income the line succumbed, to passengers in November 1948 and to freight in December 1957. One of the company's Hudswell Clarke locomotives prepares to leave Easingwold with the 1.35pm to Alne on 22 April 1935. Note the old carriage body, left, and the leaning wooden building! *W.A. Camwell*

▲ The Selsey Tramway, or to give it its full name, the Hundred of Manhood & Selsey Tramway Company Limited, opened in August 1897. The standard-gauge line ran from Chichester to Selsey and later to Selsey Beach station in what is now West Sussex. The standard-gauge line became associated with the remarkable Colonel Holman F. Stephens who ran many light railways from his offices in Tonbridge. To reduce running costs railcars were procured, which ran in 'back-to-back' mode with often a luggage/goods trailer coupled between the two. In this Chichester scene from 1923 a pair of Ford railcars are being attended to prior to departure. The quaint old line succumbed to bus competition and closed completely in January 1935. *Author's collection*

▼ Another line associated with Colonel Stephens was the Kent & East Sussex Railway, originally the Rother Valley Railway. Opened from Robertsbridge in Sussex to Headcorn in Kent in stages between 1900 and 1905, the line was built under the terms of the 1896 Light Railways Act. In 1930, a pair of petrol railcars were acquired from Shefflex Lorries Ltd of Tinsley and they ran until 1938, when they were withdrawn, being scrapped in 1941. The fascinating pair are seen at Tenterden carrying a 'K&ESR 3' identifier. Under the auspices of BR the line closed to passengers in 1954 and the last freight ran in 1961, before the preservationists moved in. *Author's collection*

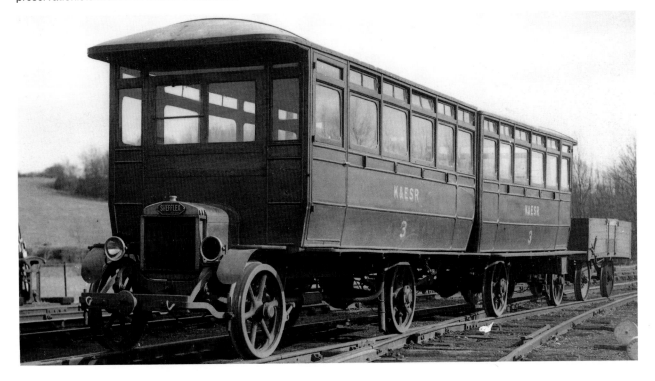

▲ The 1863 Littlehampton branch originally ran from Ford in West Sussex to the seaside town, on traditional operating principles, but later developments in 1887 saw a triangular junction created at Arundel Junction, giving the town direct access from the east, west and north. All lines were electrified in the late 1930s using the standard SR third-rail pick-up system. This view shows one of the potential problems of terminus branch stations, when on 4 August 1920, London Brighton & South Coast Railway (LBSCR) D1 class 0-4-4T No 360 suffered brake failure, running through the station retaining wall and into the adjacent road! Although often referred to as a branch, the line has a frequent service including through trains to and from London. *Author's collection*

▼ In the author's opinion there is no doubt that the two greatest British movies featuring branch lines are *Oh! Mr Porter* and *The Titfield Thunderbolt*. In the former film, Gainsborough Pictures used the SR's moribund Basingstoke & Alton Light Railway. Starring such great character actors as Will Hay, Moore Marriott and Graham Moffat the old station of Cliddesden (seen here) took on the identity of 'Buggleskelly' in Northern Ireland. In this comic view, Will Hay (Stationmaster William Porter) is being told by the local postman 'You're wasting your time' in planting lobelia on the platform. The line was another built under the 1896 Light Railways Act, opening in 1901. It was a loss-maker from the start and was closed and lifted in 1916. However, it was relaid and reopened in 1924 only to close to passengers in 1932 and to goods in 1936, except for stubs at either end. Towards the end of its life, Cliddesden station sold three tickets per week and train loadings averaged five passengers! *Author's collection*

1940s AND NATIONALISATION

THE CONDITION OF THE RAILWAYS following the end of hostilities of the Second World War was poor. During the 1939 to 1945 period the railways of the UK had provided a vital service of transportation lifelines to the nation. Around the world railways had played an important role during times of warfare, from the American Civil War onwards. In the UK the railways were essential for the transportation of goods, armaments and troops. Enemy forces realised that if they could disable the railways of the UK they would gain tactical advantage. The development of aircraft between the First and Second World Wars had been significant and by 1939/40 heavy bombers were capable of carrying substantial payloads. During 1940 and 1941, in particular, many of our great cities and the railways that served them suffered badly as a result of constant air raids. Herculean efforts were made to keep the trains running, as often, severe damage had to be repaired quickly to keep the country moving.

As a matter of historical interest, in Victorian times governments and the War Office had realised the potential of railways to increase military mobility and to help defend the country. There was once even a proposal for a London ring route to carry armoured trains conveying artillery, a sort of 4ft 8½in-gauge M25! Only the road version ever came to fruition. A military presence often resulted in the construction of railway branch lines, examples being as far apart as Devonport near Plymouth in Devon and Rosyth on the River Forth in Scotland. Inland bases and ordnance depots throughout the country often had dedicated branch lines or at least lengthy sidings and many survive to this day with regular visits by trains carrying Ministry of Defence traffic. Such examples can be found at Marchwood on the Fawley branch, Ashchurch in Gloucestershire, Kineton near Fenny Compton in Warwickshire, Bicester in Oxfordshire, Longtown and Eastriggs near Carlisle, Shoeburyness in Essex and several others. During the First World War the number and therefore frequency of passenger trains was restricted. This was not only to conserve valuable resources but it became a necessity caused by 45 per cent of all railwaymen answering the call of the country by enlisting in the armed forces.

There were many additional pressures on the railways, and by way of a single example, the extraordinary need to move coal in volume from South Wales to Grangemouth in Scotland to fuel the ships of the Royal Navy based at Scapa Flow in the Orkney Islands. This resulted in over 13,000 coal trains being operated between August 1914 and March 1919. There was naturally, a huge number of other out-of-course workings nationwide, simply to meet the requirements of the military machine during times of war. These included everything from troop trains to ambulance trains, where branch lines served a number of military hospitals, such as Netley near Southampton. As already mentioned a handful of lines closed completely during the First World War and some never reopened, for example Fratton to Southsea, the Pentewan Railway in Cornwall, the Bideford, Westward Ho! & Appledore Railway in Devon, and the Greenwich Park branch in London.

At the beginning of the Second World War the railways were financially stretched. The 'Big Four' had inherited a large backlog of works at the time of the Grouping in 1923 and with all the problems mentioned in the last chapter, they were ill-prepared for the extra work that they would be expected to undertake in a major conflict. Planning for war started in 1937 when a Railway Technical Committee was formed. The cost of implementing their recommendations was put at £5.25 million but the Government stumped up only £3.25 million to the 'Big Four'. In 1938, a Railway Executive Committee was formed to act as a link between the Government and the railway companies. The preparations for war were extensive but one of the main problems was operating with hugely dimmed or non-existent lighting to illuminate carriages and platforms. There were also manning problems but not as bad as experienced in the First World War because railwaymen were included in a schedule of reserved occupations. However, provisions were made to ensure that only skilled and experienced railwaymen were exempted from military service.

On 1 September 1939, shortly before the outbreak of war, the Government took control of the railways. Complex financial arrangements were imposed, including standard maintenance costs and a derisory total war damage allowance of £10 million. Privately owned wagons were requisitioned. At a time when railway company income would diminish they were expected to meet all of the usual operating costs and as if to rub salt in the wounds, a 1941 budget called for restrictions on price increases including rail fares and the charges for goods carried by rail. Overall, the shareholders were considerable losers, as in the background the threat of nationalisation was ever present. In practical terms one of the first high-profile uses of the railways was the evacuation of children away from our major cities. No other form of transport could have coped with such an exodus and almost

▲ Another idyllic scene, this time on the classic Lyme Regis branch in Devon and Dorset. The single-line branch from the LSWR main line at Axminster was famous for playing host to 1882-built Adams 0415 class 4-4-2T locomotives that had been put out to grass by the SR. In this pre-Second World War scene, No 3488 stands at the terminus with its single composite brake coach. How many passengers would join the train at the only intermediate station of Combpyne? Note the cattle pen in the foreground and the private coal wagons behind. The line was a victim of the Beeching axe, closing in November 1965, single-car diesel units having failed to save the line (see page 70). *W.A. Camwell*

▼ The passing of the Light Railways Act enabled the railway builders to construct their permanent way to less rigorous standards compared with the specifications of a normal railway line, but subject to certain operating restrictions. This included a maximum axle load and train speed etc. Such a 'light' railway ran from Kelvedon on the London to Norwich main line down to Tollesbury in Essex, featured here. Opening in 1904 the line was extended to Tollesbury Pier in 1907. The scene shows another aspect of branch line operations; the 'mixed' train where both passenger coaches and goods wagons would be conveyed in a single working. A Great Eastern Railway tank engine approaches Tiptree, famous for jam production, with a mixed train in the early years of operation. The line closed to passengers in 1951 and to goods in 1962, the pier having been abandoned in 1921. *Author's collection*

every British branch line was to play an important part in what turned out to be a very emotional exercise. Just to give scale to the operation in the early days of the war, over 600,000 evacuees left London in over 1,500 trains in three working days. In Liverpool, 162,000 departed in over 380 trains, with over 100,000 leaving from Glasgow and Manchester respectively. In the meantime the railwaymen on rural branches received a minor benefit when in 1939 protracted wage negotiations awarded them the princely sum of £2 7s per week (£2.35).

There were further evacuations from coastal towns in 1940 when it seemed invasion was likely and although the story of Britain's railways at war is not for this book, the remarkable efforts of the railway companies following the Dunkirk evacuation should at least be mentioned. Travel by rail was significantly more dangerous than it had been in the First World War. It is said that as the war continued the railway became battered, war-weary and less attractive. Standards of cleanliness dropped and maintenance schedules were extended, reflecting shortages of skilled workshop staff and materials, plus the use of workshops for munitions production. The permanent way was not helped by the 're-plating' of wagons whereby goods wagons were authorised to carry heavier loads than hitherto, but without compromising safety. Goods traffic on the railways increased by over 50 per cent and goods train mileage grew by nearly 20 per cent. Branch line casualties, at least in terms of traffic, were those lines that served seaside resorts where a significant holiday trade had been built up before the war. Between 1940 and 1945 locations from Filey to Newquay and from Morecambe to Great Yarmouth suffered from a complete absence of summer season holiday trains. More women were employed on the railways in a range of capacities as more railwaymen joined the armed forces.

Some branch lines served the country in a unique way. For example, the Kemp Town branch in Brighton had been a freight-only line since 1933 but a major part of its length comprised Kemp Town Tunnel. At 1,024 yards it was ideal for stabling rolling stock that would otherwise be susceptible to attack by the Luftwaffe. Branch closures during the war years were not excessive, but lines such as the remote Lybster to Wick, Moniaive to Dumfries, Oxenholme to Arnside, Shackerstone to Loughborough, Alcester to Bearley, Hay to Pontrilas, the Weston, Clevedon & Portishead Railway, and many others all closed.

Despite the damage incurred and the many trials and tribulations encountered, the railways survived the war but in a dire state. Natural resources were at rock bottom and the railways simply could not get their hands on the basic materials to regenerate their systems. In 1946, the Ministry of Supply adjudicated over the supply of materials within a country that was technically bankrupt. It is said that engines, carriages, track, signals, stations, bridges and other infrastructure items were in a terrible state, having been substantially neglected for over six years. On some

London Midland & Scottish branch lines it was impossible to see through the windows of carriages and it became necessary for passengers to open compartment doors to see whether there was an empty seat available. These were bleak days and circumstances were not helped by the appalling 1946/47 winter when transportation systems were paralysed for lengthy periods. At this time political influences were brought to bear as the Labour Party was intent on widespread nationalisation of most of the UK's major industries. There also seemed to be a majority of railway employees who favoured public ownership, which was approved by Parliament with the passing of the 1947 Transport Act, with the shareholders, who had risked their capital over many years, coming off very badly indeed.

It was not only the railways that were nationalised from 1 January 1948, but certain ports, road haulage firms, bus companies, airlines, ferries and even railway hotels. The new 'British Railways' took over 19,000 route miles of track. In the new structure 'Regions' took over from the 'Big Four' but with the London & North Eastern Railway being divided into Eastern, North Eastern and Scottish Regions, and the London Midland & Scottish Railway into the London Midland Region and Scottish Region. Operations were under the control umbrella of the British Transport Commission (BTC), an unwieldy organisation with nearly 700,000 staff. As mentioned in the Introduction, a structure for delegated responsibility was imposed by the BTC with the Railway Executive trading under the 'British Railways' label. The BTC also appointed a Branch Line Committee in 1949 with the objective of identifying branch lines that were little used and that were incurring the greatest losses.

In the early days of nationalisation there was little change on branch and minor lines as the country and the railways slowly recovered from the war years. Some branch locomotives dated back to the days of Queen Victoria and the coach or two that they hauled could, in many cases, pre-date the 1923 Grouping. Fortunately for the new British Railways organisation, steam locomotives were robust machines where tolerances were generous enabling worn-out motive power to continue providing a service, especially in the less-stressful branch line environment. In many far-flung corners of the national network locomotives continued to show their 'Big Four' liveries with only the occasional appearance of a renumbered British Railways-liveried locomotive. In general terms the new numbering system was allocated in ranges on a regional basis with the Western Region being allocated 1 to 9999, diesel locomotives 10000 to 19999, electric locomotives 20000 to 29999, Southern Region 30000 to 39999, London Midland Region 40000 to 59999, the Eastern Region 60000 to 69999, and Standard BR steam locomotives 70000 to 99999. Scottish Region locomotives were in the LMR/ER/BR Standard ranges.

There were some early casualties under the new nationalised BR organisation. Closures in 1949/50 included the Haddington branch to the east of Edinburgh, the Meltham branch near Huddersfield in Yorkshire, Bedlington to Morpeth, the Bothwell branch to the east of Glasgow, Ladybank to Mawcarse, Leysdown to Queenborough on the Isle of Sheppey in north Kent, Malton to Driffield in north Yorkshire, Mold to Brymbo, the Peebles branch from Symington, Pickering to Seamer, the Whithorn branch in Wigtown, and many others. Further closures took place in the following year and it was clear that as a result of an attack on loss-making routes many well-established branch lines were doomed.

Thus started the 50-year BR era, which would be plagued by perpetual political interference and repeated attempts to modernise the railways in order for them to become profitable. This interference would probably have been less had the railways been profit generators, but as an organisation that consumed vast Government (and therefore taxpayer) subsidies the railways were the subject of constant attention. BTC and BR had inherited a well-worn creaking system that had its roots back in the days of steam-driven, labour-intensive operations. The trade unions continued to resist change to existing outdated shift patterns/rosters, over-manning, rigid lines of demarcation, perpetual requests for better pay and conditions (to some

extent justified but subsequently more inflationary), and in later years, opposition to driver-only operation, the proposed elimination of a second man on modern traction, and the ridiculous rejection of single manning on high-speed trains running at over 100mph. Strikes, disputes and 'industrial action' continue to plague the industry and over the years have lost it hundreds of millions of pounds (and many customers), with the hugely inconvenienced travelling public usually being the innocent victims.

Such Luddite thinking belonged to the past, a view supported by the judiciary in test cases where the employer had imposed change within their organisations. Over the years many commercial customers have, unfortunately, abandoned the railways on the grounds of cost, speed and reliability, such as the newspaper industry and most of the Royal Mail, although privatisation has also seen some new freight contracts won by the railways. But here, we are concerned only with British Railways and the BTC at the beginning of the 1950s as they attempted to overcome the impact of war and modernise the railways of Britain, despite having found themselves between a rock (the Government) and a hard place (the unions).

▼ A number of branch line termini had grandiose station buildings while others had modest wooden-framed structures covered with sheets of corrugated iron. Some had other adornments such as all-over roofs. This fine example was located at Callington at the end of the branch line from Bere Alston. Built along part of the old East Cornwall Minerals Railway alignment the branch opened in 1908. Although built by the Plymouth Devonport & South Western Junction Railway the underlying capital was provided by the LSWR. The branch was absorbed by the SR at the 1923 Grouping. The line was cut back to Gunnislake in 1966, but difficult topography in the area saved the line from closure. This view dates from 5 October 1949. Of interest is the diminutive signal cabin. *Author's collection*

▶ Great Eastern Railway branch lines covered just about the whole of East Anglia like a spider's web. With a sparse rural population most of the branches and cross-country lines were loss-makers and ripe for closure under the terms of 'Reshaping Plan' criteria. Many of the branches employed elderly locomotives and stock, such as this Holden E4 class 2-4-0 No 2784. The class dated back to Victorian times, being introduced from 1891. The scene is Bartlow on 16 April 1949 with the 1.15pm train from Cambridge to Marks Tey about to depart. The line closed in 1967. Another branch connected Bartlow with Audley End, but that also closed, in 1964. *W.A. Camwell*

▼ One of the all-time greats in terms of cross-country lines was the Midland & Great Northern Joint line, which ran from Peterborough to Yarmouth, with lines to Saxby via Spalding, and to Cromer and Norwich from Melton Constable. In total the M&GN amounted to about 180 route miles and in addition to local trains a number of long-distance services were operated, especially from the East Midlands. This wonderful scene shows 1884-built Worsdell F4 class (modified by Holden) 2-4-2T No 7153 leaving the original Holt station with an amazing array of vintage coaches forming the 10.25am Melton Constable to Cromer Beach service on 17 May 1948. Most of the M&GN network closed in 1959, but Holt now has a new station belonging to the North Norfolk Railway, with trains working to and from Sheringham. The locomotive was three years older than the line itself, which opened in 1887! *SLS*

◀ The M&GN was formed in 1893 as an amalgamation of several small companies. Later operated jointly by the LNER and the LMS the cross-country lines were always secondary and therefore vulnerable in any profit-and-loss or line duplication review. Showing considerable LMS influence in this early days of BR image is a Yarmouth-bound train headed by an Ivatt 2-6-0 running tender first, pausing at the delightfully named Potter Heigham station. The signalbox operated a mixture of somersault and upper quadrant semaphore signals. The line closed from 2 March 1959. *W.A. Camwell*

◀ This architectural gem was at Richmond, North Yorkshire, on a branch from Eryholme Junction on the East Coast Main Line, with passenger services running to and from Darlington. The North Eastern Railway line ran through Catterick Bridge, where there was a connection to the large Catterick Camp army installation. Here, inside-cylinder Robinson A5 class 4-6-2T No 69837, with 'British Railways' stencilled on the side tanks, leaves the splendid terminus, with a motley rake of stock bound for Darlington. The line closed to passengers in March 1969 and to goods the following year. *JWA/SLS*

◀ Another Great Eastern Railway old-timer in the shape of E4 class 2-4-0 No 62781, but this time at the terminus of Mildenhall in Suffolk, north-east of Cambridge. The ancient ensemble is forming the 5.48pm to Cambridge on a sunny 18 April 1949. The station building style is similar to Southminster and other GER termini. The branch was 7¼ miles long to the junction at Fordham on the Ely to Newmarket line and 20¾ miles from Cambridge. The branch closed to passengers in 1962 and two years later all goods services were also withdrawn. *W.A. Camwell*

▶ Photographs taken during the Second World War are uncommon because film and processing materials were hard to come by, and there were also security implications. In this atmospheric view an Easingwold Railway warning sign frames a somewhat primitive scene with a tank engine simmering in front of a single vintage coach. Goods wagons can be seen in the yard on the right and one wonders what income may have been derived from the handful of enamel advertising boards on the left-hand fence. The railway regularly hired motive power from the LNER, usually elderly tank locomotives. This scene has been history for well over half a century (also see page 20). *W.A. Camwell*

▶ This wonderful study will be of immense interest to students of railway architecture. This ornate structure is the Caledonian Railway's Brechin station on 6 July 1951. Having been operated by the LMS for a period of 25 years, it was by then part of British Railways. Note the period BR lorry and an advertisement for Runabout tickets in order to 'see the surrounding country'. Passenger services ceased in 1952 although freight traffic continued until 1981. *W.A. Camwell*

▶ There were two branch lines that ran directly from the city of Hull to the North Sea coast, to Hornsea and Withernsea. The branches were 15½ and 20¾ miles long respectively and both closed to passengers in October 1964. Goods facilities were subsequently withdrawn. With the foreground railwayman in traditional uniform and with gas lighting extant, Raven Class A7 4-6-2T No 69796 is seen at the head of a relief holiday train at Hornsea, which comprises what appears to be a scratch rake of rolling stock, on 2 August 1949. Note the splendid station roof and wide board crossing. *W.A. Camwell*

◄ After the war years most locomotives were in a particularly grubby state and many pre-nationalisation liveries survived the advent of BR by a considerable margin. This was certainly the case with Worsdell G5 class 0-4-4T No 7315 (BR No 67315), seen in LNER livery on 7 May 1948 at Alston terminus. The train is about to depart from the smoke-stained overall roof with the 2.20pm for Haltwhistle. The 13-mile Alston branch opened in 1852 and was unlucky not to survive, being closed as late as May 1976. A narrow-gauge tourist line, the South Tynedale Railway, now operates on part of the old trackbed. *W.A. Camwell*

◄ Wells in Somerset had two stations, Tucker Street owned by the GWR, and Priory Road, the branch terminus of Somerset & Dorset Railway services from Glastonbury & Street. In this scene the 1.10pm from Yatton comes to a halt at Wells Tucker Street on a wet 5 November 1949 behind Collett 0-4-2T No 1430. Services on the Yatton to Witham line were withdrawn in September 1963. A charming sign points passengers to the 'Parcels Office and Cloak Room'. *SLS*

◄ This exceedingly rare shot shows the branch goods train at Abbeydore on the Pontrilas to Hay branch. The line lost its passenger service in December 1941 but goods traffic struggled on until the 1950 to 1953 period, services being withdrawn in geographical stages. On 21 June 1951, No 5818, one of the attractive but ubiquitous Collett 0-4-2T locomotives, is seen on a goods train for Pontrilas. A total of 95 locomotives were built in the 1400 and 5800 classes, but 1933-built No 5818 was not one of those fitted for push-pull branch line passenger services. *W.A. Camwell*

▶ This delightful branch train was photographed at Little Kimble, between Aylesbury and Princes Risborough, on 5 October 1948. No 1426 and its auto coach were forming the 12.37pm from Aylesbury, on the single-track link between the former Great Central Railway main line (now the Marylebone to Aylesbury line) and the GWR 'Birmingham Direct' route. The 7¼-mile link survives to the present time. In pre-Grouping days the line carried the label the 'Great Western and Great Central Joint Line'. *W.A. Camwell*

▶ Kemble in Gloucestershire on the Swindon to Gloucester 'Golden Valley' route was once the junction for two branch lines that served the towns of Cirencester and Tetbury, respectively. The Tetbury branch opened in 1889 and in 1901 the population of the town was only 1,989, compared with 7,536 for Cirencester. Both branches closed to passengers in April 1964 although goods trains continued to serve Cirencester Town station until the following year. In this typical branch line scene, 0-4-2T No 1436 simmers at Tetbury with the 10.35am from Kemble on 4 October 1949. *W.A. Camwell*

▶ Located 251 miles from London was the Cardiganshire terminus of Aberayron, seen here. Passenger services from Lampeter were withdrawn as long ago as September 1951, although milk trains served Green Grove siding at Felin Fach until the mid-1960s. An 0-6-0PT slumbers with a single coach at the corrugated-iron-sided station building, while in the background goods traffic would seem to be remarkably buoyant. The Commer lorry of Messrs Marsh & Baxter Ltd dates the photograph, while a contrast in oil lamp function is food for thought. *W.A. Camwell*

◀ This photograph has the atmosphere of the steam age as a combination of mist, smoke and steam generate a large dose of nostalgia. The north Kent terminus of Sheerness on Sea was photographed on 8 October 1948 and features H class 0-4-4T No 1309 (later BR No 31309) on compartment stock forming the 10.39am to Sittingbourne. The footplate crew pose for 'Cam' Camwell, one of the most prolific branch line photographers in the history of railway photography. The line was electrified as part of the Kent Coast scheme of the late 1950s and is unusual in that both passenger and freight trains continue to traverse the branch. Nearby was the abandoned Sheppey Light Railway to Leysdown. *W.A. Camwell*

◀ As the crow flies Allhallows-on-Sea was only a short distance away from Sheerness, but by rail the journey was lengthy. The Allhallows branch did not open until 1932 as a short spur from the Hoo Junction to Port Victoria line. It was thought that the area would develop into a popular resort, but it proved difficult selling plots of land on the flat and often bleak marshland. After the Second World War traffic declined and by 1961 the line was defunct. The freight-only branch to nearby Grain remains open. Here, one of the last-surviving R class 0-4-4Ts, No 31666, which was push-pull fitted, heads the 3.22pm to Gravesend Central on 7 October 1949. The scenery behind the running-in board is uninspiring. *W.A. Camwell*

◀ The Second World War had been declared when this photograph was taken at New Romney & Littlestone on Sea on 23 March 1940. Prior to the Grouping the branch was operated by the South Eastern & Chatham Railway (SECR) but here it is an LBSCR locomotive in the shape of D3 class 0-4-4T No 2363 that is heading a train to Ashford. The line succumbed in March 1967, although part of the branch is still used for traffic to Dungeness nuclear power station. Nearby is the popular 15in-gauge Romney Hythe & Dymchurch Railway. *SLS*

▲ This really delightful branch line scene depicts Kingsley Halt on the LSWR Bentley to Bordon branch on 1 June 1947. In typical post-war condition grubby M7 class 0-4-4T No 60 (shortly to become No 30060) heads for the terminus a short distance from the military town. At Bordon there was a connection with the Longmoor Military Railway, but that was insufficient to save the line, which closed to passengers in September 1957, and to goods in 1966 with the military line closing in 1969. The Bordon branch is one of the few closed lines where possible future reopening has been suggested, although who would sign the cheques has yet to be decided! *Author's collection*

▼ One of the strangest branch lines in terms of construction date, commercial purpose and potential loadings was the Halwill Junction to Torrington (and Barnstaple) line. The circuitous route that seemed to avoid most villages and hamlets was not opened until 1923. It enjoyed the rather grand name of the North Devon & Cornwall Junction Light Railway. For much of its life the service comprised just two trains per day in each direction, a prime candidate for closure by the 1950s. Shown here is a delightful mixed train, which would appear to comprise a single coach, a couple of clay wagons, and a brakevan. The ensemble is headed into Halwill Junction by E1/R class 0-6-2T No 2095 (BR No 32095), a 1927 Maunsell rebuild of a Stroudley E1 class, with a larger-capacity coal bunker. The line closed to passengers in March 1965. *Author's collection*

1950S AND MODERNISATION

THE RAILWAY EXECUTIVE WAS FACED with a monumental task in restoring the railways to any sort of normality. They continued to run services nationwide and it must never be forgotten that whatever the era, war years included, the railways carried millions of passengers every day of the week and continued to transfer goods and freight of every description to many far-flung corners of the network. One of the first activities was to reconvert the great railway works from munitions and military vehicle manufacture to traditional activities. This was no easy task after so many years of multi-tasking. Urgent consideration needed to be given to the motive power scene and a new generation of locomotives was required for both main lines and branch lines and for passenger, freight and mixed traffic working nationwide.

Most of the major pre-nationalisation companies had dabbled with diesel traction before the war but except for a single experiment had confined their activities to shunting locomotives and railcars. After the Second World War both the London Midland & Scottish Railway and the Southern Railway had recognised that following success in the USA and Germany, the future direction for main line locomotion on non-electrified lines was with diesel traction. Both companies had made rapid progress in conjunction with the English Electric company and other potential suppliers in converting design drawings into actual prototype locomotives. The first example, No 10000, a Derby-built 1,600hp 131-ton heavyweight resting on Co-Co bogies, appeared just before nationalisation towards the end of 1947. This was followed in 1948 by No 10001. The next delivery was in 1950 for the SR. An Ashford-built 135-ton 1 Co-Co 1 locomotive, No 10201, was followed by No 10202 in 1951. The history of main line diesel locomotives is detailed in the companion volume *The Rise and Fall of British Railways: Main Line Diesel Locomotives*.

Notwithstanding these trials the railway equipment inventory inherited by British Railways included thousands of steam locomotives. There was no question of abandoning steam traction and indeed most of the engineering skills within the railway workforce were based on traditional equipment and practices. The only way that there could have been a rapid dieselisation process would have been the importation of machinery from abroad, and in the post-war years of high unemployment with British industry trying to implement such a policy would have been unthinkable, not to mention politically suicidal. Furthermore, the UK could simply not afford to import thousands of locomotives. There were other issues. BR was formed long before the advent of North Sea oil exploration and blanket dieselisation would have resulted in the importation of huge amounts of fuel from sources that were not always reliable. However, there were hundreds of operational coal mines producing millions of tons of a natural resource that had powered our trains for generations. There was also the question of further unemployment in the coal industry if the 'contract' to supply large amounts of fuel for the national railway industry had been lost.

Consequently, the BTC decided that there was a future for steam traction and new BR 'Standard' designs were developed, under the oversight of R.A. Riddles. These Standard locomotives ranged from small, 2-6-2 tank engines for branch and minor line use to large 2-10-0 freight locomotives. The standard classes were mainly simple, two-cylinder machines, with good access to key areas for daily maintenance, plus a parts interchangeability policy to effect economies in both the manufacturing and stores areas. Some of these classes were based on the more efficient pre-war designs with a leaning towards LMS Ivatt and Stanier types. Also, it must not be forgotten that many of the 'Big Four' designs for both main line and branch line use continued to be manufactured after the war, with such locomotives outnumbering the BR Standard types built.

Between 1948 and 1960, British Railways built 2,537 steam locomotives in their workshops, 1,538 to traditional pre-war designs, and from 1951, a total of 999 steam locomotives to the new Standard specifications. While the decision to build steam locomotives was, in the circumstances, understandable and politically expedient, the BTC realised that long term, dieselisation and further electrification was the only way forward. Future decisions and policies resulted in some of the Standard classes of steam locomotive having a life of only five to six years. The last steam locomotive was built in 1960 with steam finally disappearing from the BR scene in 1968, the last steam-hauled branch trains being to Lymington and Kensington Olympia, respectively.

Returning to the 1950s, this was to be the decade of change although many would regard it as the decade of waste and missed opportunities. The early 1950s were spent clearing the enormous backlog of maintenance work previously referred to. This gargantuan task should not be underestimated as years of neglect in almost every operational and infrastructure department required remedial action. In the absence of significant capital investment in the railways the annual operating balance

▲ With so many closed branch lines illustrated it is refreshing to show a Yorkshire branch that closed to passengers in January 1962 but which was subsequently preserved and successfully reopened for public use. On 15 August 1959 Ivatt 2MT 2-6-2T No 41325 is seen at Oxenhope with a push-pull service for Keighley. Goods services continued for a further six months before being withdrawn in June 1962. Now preserved as the Keighley & Worth Valley Railway, the line was used for the filming of the original hugely popular *The Railway Children* film and continues to prosper. *Gavin Morrison*

▼ A long, 32¾-mile minor line that survived until 1960 was from Macclesfield (Hibel Road) station to Uttoxeter via Leek. Stopping trains took about 1 hour 14 minutes for the journey. Fowler 2-6-4T No 42421 has steam to spare with the 2.50pm ex-Uttoxeter as it approaches Cliff Park Halt on 30 September 1959. The driver was Les Beard and the fireman Phillip Green; how's that for detail? This section of track closed to passengers towards the end of 1960 and to freight in June 1964. *Michael Mensing*

◀ Another single-coach train on a lightly used line but this time at Rawtenstall in Lancashire. Aspinall Lancashire & Yorkshire Railway 2P 2-4-2T No 50647 of 1889 vintage heads the 10.25am Bury (Bolton Street) to Bacup on 4 August 1953. In 1901 the population of Bury was 58,000, Rawtenstall 31,000 and Bacup 22,000, so there was, presumably, no shortage of potential travellers. Nevertheless, the line from Bacup to Rawtenstall closed to passengers in December 1966 and from Rawtenstall to Bury (Bolton Street) in June 1972. The East Lancashire Railway now operates over part of the route. *W.A. Camwell*

◀ A family hopefully enjoying their Lake District holiday all have their overcoats on despite the summer season. The scene is the former Furness Railway Windermere Lakeside station with a visible cross-platform connection to a waiting lakeside steamer. During the 1950s, Fowler 4MT 2-6-4T No 42376 waits at the terminus with a departure for Ulverston, 9¼ miles away. Opened in 1869, the line had closed to passengers back in September 1938 but summer excursions continued to run until September 1965. The line reopened in 1973 under the auspices of the Lakeside & Haverthwaite Railway. *W.A. Camwell*

◀ This wonderful last day of service scene, on 15 June 1959, shows the former LNWR station of Birdingbury on the route from Rugby (Midland) to Leamington Spa (Avenue). A crowd wait on the platform and one lady has both a bouquet of flowers and a union flag in her hands. On the smokebox door of Ivatt 2MT No 41227 a chalk inscription 'Oh Sir Brian' has been scrawled, referring to the then BR Chairman Sir Brian Robertson (in post from 1953 to 1961). The 7.54pm from Rugby looks to be jam-packed, a frequent occurrence at such events. *Michael Mensing*

sheets of the very early 1950s showed a modest profit, but some would argue this was not a fair representation if compared to a private commercial undertaking, especially in terms of the depreciation of fixed assets. It was recognised that there would need to be radical and costly changes to all parts of the BR empire if the business was to stand a chance of becoming viable, particularly in the face of growing competition from a resurgent road haulage industry and a growth in air travel. But it would be 1953 before the Railway Executive could devote sufficient time to future planning. A considerable amount of time was spent drawing up a Modernisation Plan, the process being slowed by the somewhat bureaucratic BTC 'by committee' structure, while in the meantime, other European countries were well advanced with repairing their war-torn railways. The plan was finally published in December 1954. There was of course little point in producing a plan unless there was a strong likelihood that such plans would be funded and that had to be a political decision, with HM Treasury playing an important part in deciding what could be afforded.

Although we are concerned here with branch and minor lines many areas of the Modernisation Plan would impact the branches, especially in terms of the trains themselves. Hindsight is a wonderful thing, but years later the Plan would be seen as an opportunity missed and in several respects (but not all), a failure. The visions were grand. The objective was to bring British Railways into the 20th century by increasing line capacity, signalling, the speed of trains and safety. The BTC was trying to redress a balance between road and rail transport, which had gradually been favouring the roads for some years. The old evergreen argument had been used that although lorries paid road fund duty they did not have to pay for their 'permanent way', in other words the roads. The BTC wanted to make the railways more attractive to both passengers and freight operators, but unfortunately they did not anticipate the growth in disposable income and the 'never had it so good years' with the commensurate rapid growth in car ownership. The areas targeted were:

Electrification of a number of principal routes.

Large-scale dieselisation and the replacement of steam locomotives.

New passenger rolling stock and freight wagons.

Resignalling and track renewal in an effort to speed up trains.

Closure of a number of duplicate and heavily loss-making lines.

The price tag put on the Plan at 1955 values was a whopping £1.2 billion (over £22 billion in current values).

However, the small print showed that this expenditure was to be spread over a period of 15 years. In the Plan the BTC stated that it was not a question of whether the nation could afford the modernisation, but whether it could afford not to modernise. The Plan stated that half of the total cost of its implementation would have been spent in any event, just keeping the railways going. Also, the BTC was looking for an early return on the investment, as much as £85 million annually. The BTC stated that it would find £400 million from within its own resources, the remainder being obtained by external borrowing. The Plan did not apply costs to individual works because no priorities had been set; however, broad brush totals were given to the various categories of expenditure.

The advantages of electrification were well established, the only downside being the high initial capital cost. The BTC allocated £185 million (all at 1955 values) to electrify part of the East Coast Main Line and from King's Cross to Hitchin and the Hertford loop, Euston to Birmingham, Crewe, Manchester and Liverpool, Great Eastern lines beyond Chelmsford to Ipswich, including the Clacton, Harwich and Felixstowe branches, Liverpool Street to Hertford and Bishop's Stortford, and the Enfield and Chingford branch lines. Also included were 190 route miles of Glasgow suburban lines and 250 route miles on the Southern Region east of a line from Reading to Portsmouth, including the whole of the Kent Coast scheme, serving Dover, Ramsgate, Folkestone and Hastings.

London, Tilbury & Southend service electrification had already been announced. The electrification work on the SR would naturally be the established third-rail dc system but it was not certain that other schemes would be 1,500 volts dc overhead or whether modern ac systems would be adopted. It was anticipated that costs might exceed the budget and that the volume of work might exceed available manpower. It was stated that if this was the case then one of the main line routes would be diesel hauled until electrification could be afforded.

It came as no surprise that the Plan would announce the end of steam traction and that there would be a massive £150 million investment in diesel power. The BTC planned not to mix diesel and steam traction and they hoped to turn successive routes and areas over to exclusive diesel haulage. They estimated that a grand total of 2,500 main line diesel locomotives would be required and £125 million was being made available for that purpose. The most curious statement was that 'designs will be standardised as much as possible'. This proved not to be the case, at least in the early days under the provisions of a 'Pilot Scheme', as a myriad of suppliers constructed the most amazing concoction of diesel-electric and diesel-hydraulic types imaginable, albeit within predetermined size and weight specifications.

One of the first areas to be designated as 'all diesel' were the lines west of Newton Abbot and all lines from Waterloo to Weymouth and Exeter. It should be mentioned that a diesel shunter programme was already under way with the objective of eliminating all shunting and trip workings by steam locomotives by 1957. A crumb of comfort to steam fans was that existing locomotive orders to the tune of £10 million would be completed and that earlier and non-standard types would be the first to be eliminated. It would be another 13 years before the last BR standard-gauge steam train ran in everyday service.

The most important aspect of the Modernisation Plan to impact branch and minor lines came under the heading of 'Rolling Stock', to which £230 million had been notionally allocated. The Plan anticipated the extinction of steam-hauled non-corridor compartment type stock. It was said that such stock tended to be used on stopping and branch line steam services that carried a heavy loss. The BTC confirmed that 'Some of these services would be abandoned in favour of road services, while diesel multiple unit trains would take over such of them as are considered to offer reasonable prospects of additional traffic when modern equipment is in use.' There was already ample evidence that diesel multiple units were extremely popular with the general public, leading to increased patronage. A building programme of 4,600 diesel railcars and multiple-unit vehicles was instigated, not just for the minor lines but for 'city-to-city expresses, secondary and cross-country services'. There would also be orders for 3,600 electric multiple-unit vehicles. It was estimated that this programme would eliminate 14,000 locomotive-hauled coaches. In spite of this programme it would be 1967 before the last steam-hauled branch train trundled off into the distance.

There was little point in making all of these changes without attention to signalling and the permanent way. This part of the scheme included everything from bridge maintenance and renewal to significant colour light signalling schemes. Curves were to be eased, junctions relaid and some speed restrictions would be lifted. Track strengthening and relaying amounted to £35 million and new and additional lines a further £25 million. Main line speeds of *at least* 100mph were the target. Telecommunications and the progressive installation of automatic train control were both on the shopping list as was Centralised Traffic Control. The total envisaged expenditure under this head was to be £105 million. Stations were scheduled for improvement and the BTC were looking forward to a cleaner railway, cleaner stations and cleaner stock, with the addition of mechanised carriage cleaning and servicing depots.

The goods and freight scene was not forgotten and £140 million was designated for the improvement of goods yards and £225 million for investment in freight wagons. A total of 150 major freight yards were to be replaced by 55 new or reconstructed central yards with some being mechanised on the hump principle. There would be rationalisation on the freight scene with old goods stations giving way to concentration yards, one of the objectives

being a reduction in trip working. The Plan called for the fitting of all wagons with a continuous brake of the vacuum type. This would speed up the entire freight business and increase line capacity. Large numbers of catch points could be eliminated and 10,000 hours of engine, train and man time would be saved every week by eliminating the need to stop to pin down or pick up brakes at the summits of gradients throughout the nation. New, four-wheeled wagons were ordered. Although much larger bogie wagons were preferred the infrastructure at most collieries could not cope with anything larger than 24.5-ton wagons. The BTC also hoped to reduce wagon turn-round time by 30 per cent. It was hoped that BTC's plans would reduce total wagon stock from 1,141,500 to 752,000, a reduction of nearly 400,000 wagons! All new orders would contribute to the elimination of all wagons with old grease-lubricated bearings, another BTC objective.

In the meantime, the introduction of early lightweight diesel units in Yorkshire was a resounding success. The public had few romantic notions about the dirty steam-hauled stock that they had been obliged to travel in. The lines from Leeds to Bradford, Harrogate and Knaresborough operated by the diesels saw an increase of 125,000 passengers between June and September 1955, producing significant additional net receipts. The cleanliness of the new units and the outstanding visibility was extremely popular and as the fleet of diesel mechanical units was delivered other economies became possible, such as the elimination of a run-round requirement at branch termini and associated track and signalling. The diesel-electric units ordered by the Southern Region were disappointing in that the carriage design was not far removed from their steam-hauled predecessors at least in terms of visibility. However, these reliable units were delivered from the mid-1950s and an early start was made in the elimination of steam on a number of branch lines in Sussex and Hampshire.

All the while, branch and minor lines were closing, long before the so-called 'Beeching era'. As a small sample, the following branches closed to passenger traffic (and some completely) in the mid- to late 1950s: Alexandra Palace to Finsbury Park in north London, Alva to Ambus in Clackmannanshire, Ludgershall to Tidworth in Wiltshire (taken over by the War Department), Ashburton to Totnes, Barnsley Court House to Cudworth, Bristol to Frome, Chepstow to Monmouth Troy, Chesterfield to Elmton & Cresswell, Denbigh to Rhyl, Crystal Palace High Level to Nunhead in south-east London, Delph to Greenfield, Dundee to Forfar north of the River Tay, East Grinstead to Lewes (part of which became the Bluebell Railway), Essendine to Stamford Town, Exeter to Heathfield (the Teign Valley line) and Newton Abbot to Moreton-hampstead, Garsdale to Northallerton via Hawes (mostly in the Yorkshire Fells), Fareham to Alton (the Meon Valley line), Guthrie to Arbroath in Angus, Headcorn to Robertsbridge (the Kent & East Sussex Railway), Higham

▲ In this March 1957 view at Coalport there has been a significant deterioration in the infrastructure since the former LNWR branch from Wellington (Salop) closed to passengers in 1952. The line struggled on for goods traffic until 1960. The locomotive, 0-6-0 pannier tank No 947x (the smokebox door numberplate is broken), is of interest in that although of GWR origin it was actually built at Swindon in 1949, after nationalisation and the creation of BR. Note the shunter controlling the point lever and the surprising survival of any form of signalling. *Geoffrey Bannister*

▼ It was not always small tank locomotives that could be found operating single-coach branch trains. In this photograph at Upton on Severn in Worcestershire, ex-Midland Railway 3F 0-6-0 No 43520 runs round its single coach, No M21186M, which had formed the 5.10pm from Ashchurch, before returning at 5.45pm. Photographed on 6 June 1959, the line closed to passengers in August 1961, to goods in 1963 with the Tewksbury end of the line finally closing to goods in 1964. *Michael Mensing*

▲ In terms of diesel railcars the Great Western Railway was ahead of its time. Over the years, a range of small self-propelled rail vehicles powered by steam, petrol and diesel had been produced by a range of manufacturers, but the 38 railcars produced for the GWR between 1934 and 1942 were by far the most advanced and the most successful. One of their regular stamping grounds was between Tenbury Wells and Kidderminster, and on 20 June 1959 No W20W is seen nearing Bewdley with the 3.05pm from Tenbury Wells. This vehicle has been preserved on the Kent & East Sussex Railway. On the right is the Severn Valley route to Bridgnorth, now also preserved. *Michael Mensing*

Ferres to Wellingborough, Hexham to Riccarton Junction in the Borders, Leamington Spa to Rugby, Southwell to Rolleston Junction, Moffat to Beattock in Dumfriesshire, Newport to Sandown on the Isle of Wight, several services in the Oldham, Lancashire, area, Petersfield to Pulborough via Midhurst, Rainford Junction to Ormskirk in the North West, Peterborough to Sutton Bridge on the old M&GN, Titley to Kington in Herefordshire, Watlington to Princes Risborough, and Yarmouth Beach to Peterborough (again part of the M&GN). This incomplete list shows the truly nationwide scale of closures during the 1950s after the publication of the Modernisation Plan. Any notion that the arrival of Dr Richard Beeching as Chairman of the British Transport Commission was in itself the sole cause of post-war branch and minor line closures is demonstrably a myth. Indeed, as already mentioned, 3,318 route miles of railway line closed between nationalisation in 1948 and the 1962 'Beeching era'.

Although line closures in the past had of course been recognised and publicised, it was the 1950s when closures became almost social occasions as the last rites were administered by the local masses on the last day of service on a particular branch. Once the closure process had been exhausted (as explained in the next chapter) notices of closure were posted at all local and junction stations. During the last week of service visitors from far afield would descend on a particular branch line and take advantage of a last chance to travel the route. Many had always intended to visit but had simply not got round to it. The last day was a very special occasion where a carnival-type atmosphere would prevail before the realities of the situation were digested. Trains were often strengthened, there would frequently be a wreath on the smokebox or cab, chalk inscriptions would sometimes be applied to the locomotive, and crowds of locals who had never used the service suddenly became railfans and lamented the imminent passing of the line. Predictions of doom and despondency were uttered by many as detonators were placed on the line to give the last train a memorable send-off. Rugby scrums formed to purchase the last ticket and the strains of 'Auld Lang Syne' pierced the cold night air.

In retrospect, this was a sad time as the grand aspirations of the original proposers of the line bit the dust with nothing but a large debit balance to show for decades of operation. The days and weeks after closure were rather sombre as for the first time the realisation hit home that the line had closed for ever. Soon, the weeds started to grow and eventually contractors arrived to rip up the track. Stations were often vandalised and gradually branch line routes returned to nature. Signs and railwayana were acquired for a few pounds or shillings and many relics became collectors' items within a few years. For example, the old London & South Western Railway booking hall clock from Port Isaac Road on the North Cornwall line was acquired after closure in 1966 for the princely sum of £2, but just under 40 years later it was sold at auction by the original purchaser for over £5,000! Endless books have been written about individual branch lines and country stations and the entire minor line scene is held with great affection in the hearts and minds of significant numbers of railway enthusiasts. Long after closure many abandoned routes were converted into footpaths and bridle/cycleways with the few surviving artefacts offering large doses of nostalgia.

Although progress was made under the Modernisation Plan, there were a significant number of failures, partly caused by an inability to identify future trends in public and business behaviour. For example, the large investment made in marshalling yards and concentration depots completely ignored the dramatic downturn in the hugely loss-making wagonload freight traffic. The ordering of diesel locomotives did not match the declared policy contained in the Plan. Classes of diesel locomotive were not standardised and millions of pounds were spent on large numbers of locomotives that were of an unproven design. In some cases repeat orders were made for locomotives that had not turned a wheel. Large numbers of low-powered diesels were ordered but with dwindling branch line passenger and freight traffic there was insufficient work for these types. The shunter procurement was a total disaster with a staggering 1,200 units being ordered with a diminishing workload nationwide. As it transpired some BR standard steam locomotives and early diesel types had a working life of just a few years before being withdrawn. Equipment and labour costs increased substantially while receipts dwindled in real terms. The promised savings were never delivered and by 1960 the railways had an operating deficit of £68 million, much to the annoyance of the Government and HM Treasury.

▼ The angular but stylish looks emanating from an art deco period are pronounced in this late afternoon view at Easton Court of 'whiskered' No W29W, on the 6.22pm Kidderminster to Woofferton on 20 June 1959. This car was built at Swindon in 1940/41. It weighed 35½ tons, had a seating capacity of 48, and was powered by two AEC 105hp diesel engines. This section of track closed to passengers in July 1961, and looking at the state of the platforms, the end was indeed nigh. *Michael Mensing*

▲ By the late 1950s, the logical successors to the GWR railcars on a number of branches were a brand-new generation of DMUs. Single power car versions from both the Gloucester Railway Carriage & Wagon Company and the Pressed Steel Company were eventually classified Classes 122 and 121 respectively. In the year after they were first produced a pair of 'Gloucesters', Nos W55004 and W55005, are seen at Dudley with the 4pm Birmingham Snow Hill working on 26 September 1959. Most single power cars (SPCs) were withdrawn in the early 1990s, but a couple of Pressed Steel examples are still in regular service, over 50 years since their construction. *Michael Mensing*

▼ A number of small, four-wheeled railbuses were designed in the 1950s and constructed for use on little-used branch lines, but any economies that were realised compared with steam power were, in the main, insufficient to save unremunerative lines from closure. This was not the case here, though, as the Braintree branch in Essex was eventually electrified, ensuring its long-term survival. Operationally these tiny units were far from successful with most lasting just a few years in service. A total of 22 two-axle railbuses were produced during 1958 by five different manufacturers, this one by Waggon und Maschinenbau of Germany. No E79961 is seen at Witham with the 3.42pm for Braintree & Bocking on 21 March 1959. It was scrapped in May 1968. *Michael Mensing*

▶ It may come as a surprise to many but despite the remoteness of some of the countryside a network of branch lines covered much of Aberdeenshire. Featured here is the Great North of Scotland Railway branch line from Maud Junction to Peterhead. Kittybrewster's B12 class 4-6-0 No 61513 is seen at the terminus with the 3.08pm to Maud Junction and Aberdeen on 6 May 1950. The line closed to passengers on 3 May 1965 and to freight on 7 September 1970, leaving this important fishing port with a population of 18,000 without any form of rail transport. *W.A. Camwell*

▶ Few would disagree that the Scottish town of St Andrews in Fife, 468 rail miles from London, is best known for its connections with the world of golf. The old North British Railway branch line closed to passengers in two sections; from Levan to St Andrews in September 1965, and from Leuchars Junction to St Andrews in January 1969. On 13 July 1955, NBR Reid Class J37 0-6-0 No 64627 passes the site of the old St Andrews station with the 11.31am from Leuchars Junction. The goods yard seems to be well populated with coal wagons. *W.A. Camwell*

▶ Another Great North of Scotland Railway branch line ran from Elgin to Lossiemouth on the Moray Firth. With the North Sea visible above the goods wagons the 1.44pm train to Elgin is about to depart behind a Victorian, Pickersgill-designed, D40 class 4-4-0, No 62267, one of the last survivors of the class. Note the words 'British Railways' on the well-stocked tender. The line was a Beeching casualty, closing to passengers in April 1964 and to goods two years later. *W.A. Camwell*

▲ Continuing the Scottish theme is this intriguing view of Fraserburgh on 2 September 1952. The 'main' branch line was 47 miles north of Aberdeen with its origins also with the Great North of Scotland Railway. This lengthy route closed to passengers, north of Dyce Junction, in October 1965 (freight October 1979) while the 5¼-mile Fraserburgh to St Combs branch line had closed five months earlier. The locomotives working the latter branch were normally fitted with a cowcatcher, an unusual practice in the UK. On 2 September 1952, F4 class 2-4-2T No 67157 of 1884 vintage leaves Fraserburgh's magnificent train shed for the St Combs terminus. *NRK/SLS*

▼ This splendid combination of diminutive tank locomotive, single composite brake coach and single four-wheeled van would be a modeller's delight. The scene is Dornoch in Sutherland, a whopping 657 rail miles from London, with a 1901 population of just 624 persons. Opened in 1902, the 7¾-mile light railway was operated by the Highland Railway prior to the 1923 Grouping. For much of its life there were just four trains per day in each direction. One of three intermediate stopping places, by request, was the delightfully named Cambusavie Platform! No 55051, a little Drummond 1P class 0-4-4T dating back to 1905, prepares to leave for The Mound on the Inverness to Wick and Thurso line in June 1960, the month of total closure. *W.A. Camwell*

▲ With a burst of regulator to compensate for the visible incline into Ravenscar station, BR standard 4MT 2-6-4T No 80117 arrives with the five-coach 4.20pm Whitby (Town) to Scarborough on 15 July 1957. The station was located on the 58-mile-long North Eastern Railway route from Middlesbrough to Scarborough, which ran along the North Sea coast for some distance, passing such well-known locations as Whitby and Robin Hood's Bay. North of Whitby the line closed completely in May 1958 and between Whitby and Scarborough in March 1965. *Michael Mensing*

▼ Crossing the River Esk at Ruswarp, less than two miles from its Whitby destination, is A8 class 4-6-2T No 69861, a Gresley rebuild of a Raven Class D 4-4-4T locomotive, with the two-coach 8.15am local from Goathland on 23 July 1958. It is refreshing to report that the line and the station are still open as part of the Esk Valley line from Middlesbrough to Whitby. In recent times dispensation has been given for the North Yorkshire Moors Railway to run their preserved locomotives and stock over this part of the route. *Michael Mensing*

▲ This busy scene from 2 August 1958 features Whitby Town station, where railway history dates back to the Whitby & Pickering Railway of 1836. At 8.18am a patched-up A8 class 4-6-2T, No 69864, is seen shunting two vans into the centre road. The 'Platform 2' departure board shows a through train for Pickering, Malton, York, Grantham and King's Cross! Note the tail lamp on the platform. Although the Whitby line has survived there is, alas, no future prospect of a through train to London. *Michael Mensing*

▼ This view shows Ravenscar Tunnel at the summit of the old 1885-built Scarborough & Whitby Railway. The climb up to the tunnel was as steep as 1 in 39. It is presently possible to walk into the tunnel with a footpath either side. Looking as though BR really did need a modernisation plan, tired-looking A8 class 4-6-2T, No 69867, heads five coaches forming the 2.20pm Scarborough to Whitby (Town) on 15 July 1957. Although an attractive run during the summer the coastline could be bleak and windswept during the long winter months. *Michael Mensing*

▶ The substantial brick-built Chard Town station with its grand commodious overall roof spanning a single platform offers immense aesthetic appeal. Projecting an image of a leisurely way of life the driver and fireman of Collett 5700 class 0-6-0PT No 5721 pose for the camera with a train that has just arrived from Taunton. The grand plans of the Victorian era were completely dashed in September 1962 when the line closed to passengers. *W.A. Camwell*

▶ There is some wild and desolate country around Craig-y-Nos on the old Neath to Brecon route. Prior to the Second World War there were only four trains a day in each direction, but the line soldiered on until October 1962. An 0-6-0PT with a pair of non-matching coaches pauses at the station in the late 1950s. There appears to be a modicum of freight traffic in the background. Part of the line, from Neath to Onllwyn, remains open as a freight-only route to a coal washery. *W.A. Camwell*

▶ Throughout the UK, branches and minor lines came in all shapes and sizes and a line that has attracted plenty of publicity over the years has been the Weymouth Quay line, sometimes referred to as the tramway. The attraction for photographers was filming the boat trains running through the streets of the town. However, there were also shunting duties to perform and in past years a moderate amount of freight traffic, much of it for the Channel Islands. On 10 March 1956, 0-6-0PT No 1370, with outside cylinders, shunts the quay watched by a small boy with a soapbox cart and an elderly gentleman carrying a dog. Services along the quay line have now been suspended. *Ray Hinton*

▲ It is easy to forget than on most branch lines it was not only passengers and freight that were conveyed, but also post and parcels. The parcels could be GPO traffic or the railway's own parcels, in later years marketed as 'Red Star'. In this 'wish you were here' scene 0-6-0PT No 6400 pauses at the Devon station of Horrabridge on the Plymouth to Launceston branch, as the train guard and station porter offload a handful of boxes, one with 'Players Please' on the side. Passenger services ceased in December 1962 and attractive scenes such as this became transport and social history overnight. *W.A. Camwell*

▼ In this intriguing photograph, two tail lamps face the photographer, attached to two different generations of diesel unit at Ledbury. On the right a GWR streamlined railcar has just arrived from Gloucester, while on the left, a green-liveried Cravens-built DMU forms a Hereford to Worcester and Birmingham service. Beyond the pair is the single-track Ledbury Tunnel beneath the Malvern Hills. The branch from Gloucester closed in July 1959, long before the arrival of Dr Beeching, but the secondary 'main line' survives. *W.A. Camwell*

▲ This superb photograph is simply bursting with interest. In addition to being a fine composition in breathtaking surroundings, points of particular note are that some 11 years after nationalisation the locomotive still has 'GWR' emblazoned on its pannier tanks, the full Blaenau Ffestiniog Central running-in board is complete, the posters invite travellers to 'park your car', even in 1959, and quite useful in North Wales, is a map of the London Underground! This charming train, headed by No 7428, had just arrived from Bala on 30 March 1959, nine months before the line closed. In later years, nuclear traffic worked along the branch to the power station at Trawsfynydd. *Gavin Morrison*

▼ This photograph shows the same train as illustrated in the view above, justified by an incredibly animated scene and typical Welsh topography. The footplate crew are busy at the intermediate station of Trawsfynydd watering their trusty steed in the shape of No 7428, a youngster boards the train, while another schoolboy with mandatory cap wanders towards the single coach. A charming touch is the lady passenger having a chat with the guard. Such scenes have now gone for ever but the camera has saved the moment for posterity. The train would take 1 hour 15 minutes to cover the 24¾ miles from Blaenau Ffestiniog to Bala, an average speed of 19.8mph! *Gavin Morrison*

▲ From the mountains of Wales to the mountains of Scotland, our intrepid photographer has moved on to the Aberfeldy branch, the terminus of an 8¾-mile line from Ballinuig on the Perth to Inverness main line. The track layout in this view illustrates the classic run-round loop. On 13 June 1959, ex-Caledonian Railway McIntosh-designed 2P 0-4-4T No 55218 and its two maroon coaches are about to leave the Perthshire town for the junction station. Services were withdrawn from 3 May 1965. *Gavin Morrison*

▼ More mountains as a backcloth, but this time at Killin in Perthshire. 'Caley' 0-4-4T No 55173 is ready to leave for Killin Junction on 10 August 1960. Before closure in September 1939 passengers could continue beyond Killin to Loch Tay; however, by September 1965, there would be no passengers as the entire line closed, along with the Callander to Crianlarich 'main' line following a landslip near Glenoglehead. The old wooden station looks dilapidated, but according to the sign the public telephone was working. *Gavin Morrison*

▶ Another single-coach branch train, but this time in the garden of England. Crossing an ungated minor road at Frittenden Road station is aged O1 class 0-6-0 No 31065 with a Headcorn Junction to Tenterden working. Photographed on 13 August 1952, this section of the Kent & East Sussex Railway would close completely from 1 January 1954. This old locomotive started life as a Stirling South Eastern Railway Class O, introduced in 1878, but it was rebuilt by Wainwright in 1903. It survived the cutter's torch and is now a resident of the Bluebell Railway. *T.C. Cole*

▶ The H class 0-4-4T locomotives were for many years the mainstay of branch lines in the counties of Kent and East Sussex. They were the SECR equivalent of the LSWR M7 class. In this 1950s view, No 31263 has just arrived at the terminus of Hawkhurst at the end of the 11½-mile branch line from Paddock Wood. The station building has a Colonel Stephens influence. The line was opened in 1892 and it closed throughout in June 1961. In its heyday and in the season, the branch was well known for hop-picker specials, with allegedly 10,000 Londoners arriving in a single day. *Author's collection*

▶ In railway history terms, Midhurst in West Sussex was remarkable in that it was served by three separate branch lines, from the east, west and south. The line to Chichester closed to passengers in 1935 (although the southern end remained open for goods traffic until 1991). The lines to Petersfield on the Portsmouth direct line and to Pulborough on the Mid-Sussex line both closed to passengers in February 1955. Goods services disappeared from Midhurst and Petworth in 1964 and 1966 respectively. Here, M7 class 0-4-4T No 30048 arrives at Midhurst with a train from Petersfield in 1953. *W.A. Camwell*

◄ The LSWR Class O2 0-4-4Ts were purposeful little tank locomotives that found work on the railways of the Isle of Wight. They were not displaced until 1966, by which time many of the island lines within what had been a 55-route-mile network had closed. The branch line from Brading to Bembridge was an early casualty, closing in September 1953, after a life of 71 years. Just four months before closure, No W14 *Fishbourne* prepares to leave for the junction at Brading. The two non-corridor coaches offer three compartments for first-class passengers. *T.C. Cole*

◄ When the author visited Bembridge station in 1970 it was boarded up and derelict. The intervening 17 years since closure had taken their toll. Although the majority of stations suffered badly after closure due to vandalism, zero maintenance and weathering, especially where the sites were remote, others were restored to form fine homes, while some were sold for subsequent commercial use. There was also always the risk of redevelopment and in this case the station was demolished shortly after this photograph was taken and replaced by new houses, some standing on the site of the 220ft-long platform. *Author*

◄ Another Kentish line closure took place on 1 August 1953, which was the last day of operation for passenger trains on the Gravesend West branch line from Farningham Road (Fawkham Junction). Performing the last rites was H class 0-4-4T No 31671, seen here at Gravesend West station. Most trains worked through from Bromley South. One of the intermediate stations was Longfield Halt, shown in Bradshaw's timetable as the station for 'Pinden and Westwood'. *Author's collection*

▲ This rural backwater is at Moorswater near Liskeard in Cornwall. Nearby was the original transshipment point where minerals brought down from the mines and quarries around Caradon Hill were transferred to barges on the Liskeard & Looe Union Canal. A railway from Moorswater to Looe opened in 1860 and passengers were carried from 1879. The line was not linked to Liskeard main line station until 1901. Passing the old Moorswater engine shed in the mid-1950s is small Prairie 2-6-2T No 4552 with a short freight. There was an active rail-served clay drying plant nearby, which closed in 1996, the site now being used for occasional deliveries of cement products. *Author's collection*

▼ The Newquay branch in Cornwall has a rich and colourful history dating back to the 1840s. Once part of the horse-operated Treffry Tramway it was not until 1874 that Newquay was connected to Par and Fowey by rail. In this 1950s view, 4500 class 2-6-2T No 4508 is seen heading a Par to Newquay local at Roche station. Roche was originally called Holywell and later Victoria, before the Roche name was applied in 1904. Roche is still open but only a single track passes a single platform and all of the buildings and the platform on the left have been swept away. *W.A. Camwell*

▲ This image is a modeller's delight with a diminutive single-coach branch train, 'Titfield Thunderbolt' locomotive (0-4-2T No 1447), goods shed, engine shed, water tower, gas lighting and with even a few milk churns on the single platform. The location is Wallingford in the Thames Valley, located at the end of a branch line from Cholsey & Moulsford. The charming branch closed to passengers in June 1959, the line having been loss-making for some time. Goods traffic lasted until 1981. Most of the track is still in situ and preserved trains traverse the rails of the Cholsey & Wallingford Railway on a number of weekends throughout the year. *R.K. Blencowe*

▼ This old locomotive, an example of the well-known 'Dean Goods' 0-6-0s of 1883 vintage, is performing duties that it was designed for. No 2516 was one the last survivors of the class (and subsequently preserved) and the old girl is seen here forming its train by shunting wagons at Kerry station in Montgomeryshire on 2 December 1955. By then the town was served by this thrice-weekly goods, passenger services having ceased way back in February 1931. The branch from Abermule on the Cambrian main line closed completely in May 1956. The weedkiller would not be required! The number is carried on a smokebox plate and is still on the bufferbeam. *Geoffrey Bannister*

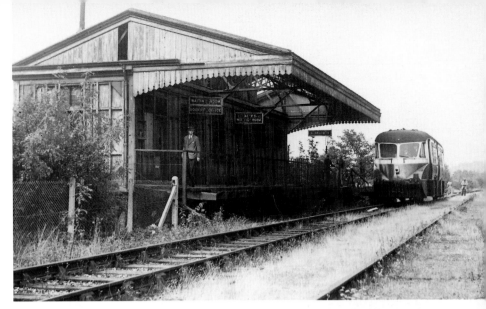

▶ It was not only rural parts that were served by branch lines, and even within 20 miles of the Capital, there were many interesting backwaters. With the abandoned GWR Uxbridge High Street station on the left a railway enthusiast special comprising a GWR streamlined railcar, pays a visit in the 1950s, while railfans explore and photograph the scene. Goods services were finally withdrawn in 1964, the last passenger train having run before the Second World War, in September 1939. *Rail Archive Stephenson*

▶ Featured here is a cross-country route that was a minor line only towards the end of its days. With just weeks to go before closure, Collett 0-6-0 No 2240 pauses at Winchester Chesil station with a train from Didcot to Southampton Terminus via Newbury. The 56¾-mile route was heavily used during the Second World War, but once hostilities had ended the service was relegated to secondary status with only four through trains per day in each direction. Passenger services along the old Didcot Newbury & Southampton Railway were abandoned in September 1962. *Author's collection*

▶ Burnham-on-Sea in Somerset was immortalised by the wonderful monochrome film made by the BBC in 1963 featuring the former Poet Laureate Sir John Betjeman CBE (1906–84). He visited the line from Highbridge to the seaside town long after the withdrawal of passenger services in October 1951, but just before goods services were axed in May 1963. Occasional excursion trains had continued to run until 1962. The line dated back to 1858 and the Somerset Central Railway when the station was just plain 'Burnham'. There were a number of operators over the years but actual closure was by the Western Region of BR. Bridgwater Bay is just beyond the high building in the left background, and until the 1880s, the line continued on to the local pier. The little signalbox on the right was restored and is now located at Washford on the West Somerset Railway. *R.E. Toop*

◄ This photograph not only encapsulates a wonderful branch line scene but depicts the fascinating subject of the mixed train, containing passengers, parcels and goods. Pausing at the original Gunnislake station on the line from Bere Alston in Devon to Callington in Cornwall, is O2 class 0-4-4T No 30183 with the 3.15pm departure on 21 September 1955. The line's engineer was the famous Colonel Stephens, and the route opened in 1908, partly on the trackbed of the 3ft 6in-gauge East Cornwall Minerals Railway (see page 26). The line from Plymouth to a new Gunnislake station to the south of this site remains open but the Callington section was abandoned in 1966. *Sid Nash*

◄ The Greenford branch from Ealing Broadway and West Ealing is still in operation, serving west London communities. In this 1950s view an auto-train is in use, which avoided the requirement for the locomotive to run round its train whatever the direction of travel. Leaving the auto-coach *Wren,* a handful of passengers have finished their day's work as they alight at Drayton Green Halt (Ealing). No 1474 will continue via Castle Bar Park Halt to Greenford. On this fine summer's day, tennis players can be seen above the up side pagoda hut. *Author's collection*

◄ The Hemyock branch from Tiverton Junction in Devon had an interesting history. Known as the Culm Valley Light Railway the locally sponsored line opened during 1876. It was built on the cheap in so far as the alignment followed the valley of the meandering River Culm. Passenger services were withdrawn in 1963. The line relied on agricultural and milk traffic for survival, although by 1975, all sources had ceased, resulting in complete closure. Here, 0-4-2T No 1451 and its single coach are seen at the Hemyock terminus in the 1950s (see page 117). *R.K. Blencowe*

▶ There are three railway lines featured in this remarkable view. The green-liveried Metropolitan Cammell DMU (introduced from 1956) is seen curving away from the Grosmont to Whitby (Esk Valley) line, just visible, as it climbs Prospect Hill to West Cliffe station, which was at an even higher level. It would then reverse in order to cross the massive 1885-built Larpool Viaduct in the right background. The train is the 1.29pm Middlesbrough to Scarborough working of 23 July 1958, which will continue through Robin Hood's Bay and Ravenscar, already featured. The line closed in March 1965. *Michael Mensing*

▶ This view from the footbridge at Bewdley station will be familiar to all fans of the Severn Valley Railway, the only difference being that this scene, from 15 August 1959, of a Birmingham Snow Hill-bound train, pre-dates the closure of the line from Shrewsbury by four years. The passenger services on both lines to the east of Bewdley, to Kidderminster and Hartlebury respectively, closed to passengers in January 1970. The introduction of DMUs was a roaring success throughout the country as the units were cleaner and the visibility considerably better compared with the old steam-hauled compartment stock. *Michael Mensing*

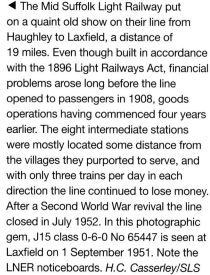

◄ The Mid Suffolk Light Railway put on a quaint old show on their line from Haughley to Laxfield, a distance of 19 miles. Even though built in accordance with the 1896 Light Railways Act, financial problems arose long before the line opened to passengers in 1908, goods operations having commenced four years earlier. The eight intermediate stations were mostly located some distance from the villages they purported to serve, and with only three trains per day in each direction the line continued to lose money. After a Second World War revival the line closed in July 1952. In this photographic gem, J15 class 0-6-0 No 65447 is seen at Laxfield on 1 September 1951. Note the LNER noticeboards. *H.C. Casserley/SLS*

◄ Well into the BR era, Great Eastern Railway branch lines in particular were operated by ancient locomotives and stock. When photographed at the junction station of Long Melford heading a Cambridge to Colchester working in 1956, this E4 class 2-4-0, No 62785, was already 65 years old. Every facility seems to have been afforded to male passengers, note the 'Gentlemen' signs on both up and down platforms, but what of the needs of the ladies? The service was withdrawn in March 1967. *Author's collection*

◄ An early photograph of Langholm station in Scotland appears on page 17. Although the branch line from Riddings was only seven miles long, all but the first down and the last up train of the day worked to and from Carlisle via Scotch Dyke, some 21¼ miles from Langholm. In this late 1950s view a commendably clean example of the numerous chunky J39 class 0-6-0s, No 64888, is seen at the terminus with a pair of maroon coaches. The branch formed a junction with the long-closed Waverley route from Carlisle to Edinburgh. *W.A. Camwell*

▶ This photograph will raise a smile with older readers when they consider the modern implications of so-called 'health and safety' regulations. The photographer on the right, in particular, would seem to be at risk of either being squashed by two large steam engines or plunging head first into the River Severn! This study shows the Severn Bridge at Sharpness with 'Castle' class 4-6-0s Nos 5018 *St Mawes Castle* and 5042 *Winchester Castle* conducting tests on 17 July 1956. The route from Lydney to Sharpness closed in October 1960 after the bridge was damaged by a runaway barge. *W.A. Camwell*

▶ Over the years there has been plenty of discussion in trying to identify when the first railway enthusiasts' special train ran. There is no doubt that what today would be called 'Chartex' specials operated before the Second World War. However, by the 1950s a combination of rapidly disappearing locomotive classes and branch and minor line closures created a potentially enormous niche railway enthusiasts market for haulage and travel, that continues to this day. The large railway clubs such as the Stephenson Locomotive Society, the Railway Correspondence and Travel Society and the Locomotive Club of Great Britain, promoted large numbers of railtours. Shortly before the line closed, swarms of railfans are seen here at Bala having spilled out of a lengthy SLS special. *W.A. Camwell*

▶ With not a pair of blue jeans or white trainers in sight, these RCTS members are having a great time at Fawley in Hampshire in 1953. Having traversed the branch from Totton many are keen to record the special event with the camera. On the left is what appears to be a 757 class 0-6-2T, while on the right is USA 0-6-0T No 30082. It is sobering to reflect that even the youngest person visible will now be at least 70 years of age. *Sid Nash*

▲ With multiple heads choosing to ignore the 'Do not lean out of the window' warning transfers, this LBSCR-based RCTS special is seen exiting Kemp Town Tunnel on the outskirts of Brighton, on 5 October 1952. Hauling a pair of auto-coaches forming set No 727, Stroudley A1X class 0-6-0T No 32636 provides the motive power. Passenger services were withdrawn in January 1933, a victim of local bus competition, but the site was used as a rail-connected coal yard until June 1971. *T.C. Cole*

▼ This is another view that clearly demonstrates that despite the nationalisation of the railways there was no hurry in certain areas to create the new identity by a livery change. More than three years after the end of the Southern Railway, Class I1X 4-4-2T No 2002 still sported the word 'Southern' on its side tanks as it emerged from Heathfield Tunnel with the 4.39pm Eastbourne to Tunbridge Wells West on 12 May 1951. The so-called 'Cuckoo Line' closed in stages, but passenger services ceased in June 1965. *Sid Nash*

▶ There are few better-looking steam locomotives that the LSWR T9 4-4-0 'Greyhounds'. Their large, 6ft 7in driving wheels were impressive and they had a good turn of speed. With its headcode discs prominent, No 30117 leaves Horsebridge with the 6.40pm Andover to Eastleigh on 22 May 1957. The line was once the southern end of Midland & South Western Junction services that ran from Cheltenham, through Andover to Southampton. The cross-country line from Andover Junction to Romsey closed from 7 September 1964. The only surviving T9 can be seen at the Bodmin & Wenford Railway in Cornwall. *R.K . Blencowe collection*

▶ It was not only steam traction that was used on special trains. On this occasion it was the Yorkshire Publicity Association that hired a six-car DMU formation for a run on the remaining section of the doomed 39¼-mile Garsdale to Northallerton line. The section from Hawes to Northallerton had closed in April 1954, but the Garsdale to Hawes section closed on this day, 16 March 1959. This was the only known DMU working to Hawes, seen on 6 September 1958, a fact probably lost on the six small boys in the driving cab. It is not known when the goods wagons were cleared. *Gavin Morrison*

▶ While some national railtours had full-length trains, those organised by regional branches were often much shorter, travelling over local lines that were on the closure list. On 12 September 1959, the SLS chartered a three-car Swindon 'Cross Country' DMU for a run on the LNWR Coalport branch line. The West Midlands tour is seen at Hadley while returning to Wellington. Again, the green livery with whiskers is featured, dating the photograph, which is now more than half a century old! *Michael Mensing*

◄ Melcombe Regis was an intermediate station on the Weymouth and Portland Joint Railway, operated by the LSWR and the GWR. Part of the route was recently in focus when in 2008/9 it was featured in the BBC Julia Bradbury presented *Railway Walks* television series. The slightly obscure and rarely photographed route closed to passengers in March 1952 and to goods in April 1965. Here, an ex-LSWR Class O2 pauses at the Dorset station on 10 October 1950. *W.A. Camwell*

◄ There may be 'trouble at t' mill' as slowly but surely over several decades the Yorkshire textile industry was decimated in the face of cheap imports manufactured in the sweat shops of the Far East. Some of the buildings and stacks have been saved for posterity by reuse, but the majority have been demolished. The topography of Holmfield in West Yorkshire is well illustrated in this April 1952 view as N1 class 0-6-2T No 69443 departs with the 12.30 Bradford Exchange to Halifax Town service. The locomotive was allocated to Bradford Hammerton Street which had a ten-track shed, that closed to steam in 1958 and to DMUs in 1984. The line closed to passengers in May 1955 and to goods in 1960. *Gavin Morrison*

◄ Market Weighton was once a major four-way railway junction with lines radiating to York, Selby, Driffield and Hull (via Beverley), but unbelievably, the town with a population of over 5,000 is now completely rail-less. Many of the old rail routes towards the north of the town are used as footpaths and cycleways. In this scene an all-green Cravens DMU forming a York to Hull service, leaves the town and passes a very impressive signal gantry topped by a formidable finial. The town lost its passenger services in 1965 and this area is now a housing estate. *W.A. Camwell*

1960s AND RATIONALISATION

BRITISH RAILWAYS LOSSES CONTINUED with an £87 million deficit in 1961 and a massive £102 million loss in 1962 (nearly £2 billion at today's values). Large sums had been spent on modernising the railway and many lines had been closed to save money, but the return on the investment never materialised, indeed, there were further moves from rail to road and air transport. It was clear that these large monolithic nationalised industries were grossly inefficient and losses were also being incurred in the nationalised energy supply industries. For example, between 1948 and 1960 over 250 coal mines closed with a loss of 100,000 mining jobs and yet the 1960 National Coal Board accounts showed a loss of £64 million, well over £1 billion at current values. Questions were asked in Parliament as to how these losses would be funded, with either the taxpayer or borrowing being the only solution. It was clear that something radical had to be done as the scale of losses could not possibly be defended, even if the railways were considered by some as a social service.

Accordingly, Harold Macmillan's Conservative Government passed the 1962 Transport Act whereby the British Transport Commission was abolished and the British Railways Board created. The then Minister of Transport, the Rt Hon. Ernest Marples MP (who had connections with the road transport industry) appointed the industrialist Dr Richard Beeching as Chairman of the Board, with remuneration of £24,000 per annum, a fortune in those now far-off days. His remit was to look closely at BR operations and to make recommendations for savings and halt the spiralling costs. His efforts turned out to be probably the most significant event between nationalisation and privatisation. The culmination of his efforts and those of his team was the publication of a report in 1963 titled *The Reshaping of British Railways* and an overview of this vital document, which was to have a devastating effect on the branch and minor lines in the UK, follows.

It was no lesser person than the Prime Minister who is quoted at the beginning of the report, effectively giving global terms of reference. He said that 'First the industry must be of a size and pattern suited to modern conditions and prospects. In particular, the railway system must be remodelled to meet current needs, and the Modernisation Plan must be adapted to this new shape.' Translated, this meant that all waste and loss-making aspects of the business had to be addressed and savings made to ensure that BR ran profitably. The report apologised for the time lapse between commencement and publication, pointing out that there had previously been no system for relevant data capture, and before anything could be done the old BTC structure had to be reorganised. It was repeated that the BRB had a duty to 'employ the assets vested in it, and to develop and modify them, to the best advantage of the nation'.

They were keen to point out that the report provided options, and choices would need to be made on the basis of such options. It would not be possible for comparative purposes to cost other forms of transport on a like-for-like basis. There were some inconsistencies; for example, it was stated that the purpose of the report was not to reject all parts of the system that did not pay or could not easily be made to pay, but on the other hand they wished to eliminate all services 'which, by their very nature, the railways were ill-suited to provide'. In other words, buses were more suitable for serving rural communities than railways. The report stated that it would look at the quality and speed of service, better operating methods, and attracting traffic, which were all expected to substantially improve the financial position. As if it would satisfy the public, the report recognised that 'changes of the magnitude of those proposed will inevitably give rise to many difficulties affecting railway staff, the travelling public, and industry'.

The report went back in time to the end of the Second World War, acknowledging what has already been discussed here, that the railways were in a poor physical state. It was pointed out that since 1952 the railways had progressively lost money. It was critical of the 1955 Modernisation Plan for 'not envisaging any basic changes in the scope of railway services or in the general mode of operation of the railway system' and went on to say that in total, the implementation of the key ingredients of the Plan had failed to make the railways pay by reducing costs and attracting more traffic.

One of the most profound statements admitted that there was considerable scope for cost reduction by a multiplicity of economies over the whole field of operations, and that vigorous efforts would be made to achieve them. Nevertheless, it was obvious, even before detailed investigation started, that neither modernisation nor more economical working could make the railways viable in their existing form, and that a reshaping of the whole pattern of the business would be necessary as well. It was stated that since nationalisation the railway business had comprised a mixture of good, bad, and indifferent routes, services and traffic. There was implied criticism of the statutory fixing of rates without having regard to true costs. The report pointed to the weaknesses of a system where there was

▲ In the far North East a branch line ran from Alnmouth in Northumberland to Alnwick, with the North Eastern Railway line continuing to Coldstream and beyond. The latter section of line closed way back in September 1930, but the three miles to Alnwick continued to be served by a passenger service until January 1968. Here, J39/1 class 0-6-0 No 64852 stands at Alnmouth on 21 May 1961 with the 5.35pm to Alnwick. Dieselisation failed to save the line. *Michael Mensing*

▼ Another line that straddled the Anglo-Scottish border ran from Tweedmouth in Northumberland via Kelso to St Boswell's in Roxburgh, on the Waverley route. Running through a thinly populated area it was perhaps surprising that passenger services lasted until June 1964, with goods services closing in stages between March 1965 and April 1968. Hauling a single coach of LNER origin, Standard 2MT 2-6-0 No 78047 heads west from Kelso with the 2.21pm to St Boswell's on 30 May 1962. *Michael Mensing*

cross-subsidisation of carrying bad traffic on the back of financially good traffic. Road traffic competition had driven down the rates the railways could charge for good traffic and it could no longer be expected to subsidise bad traffic if the railways were to run profitably.

Beeching wanted to look at the railways from a high level to determine where they could successfully operate as part of a national transport system. The report logically deduced that the provision of railways should be limited to routes over which it was possible to develop dense flows of traffic, of the kinds which lent themselves to movement in trainload quantities and which, in part at least, would benefit from the speed and reliability which the railways were capable of achieving. The financial figures and other data used in the report were from the year 1961, the latest year that fully detailed cost data was available. Total railway income in terms of gross receipts was £475 million and working expenses were £562 million, a net deficit of £87 million. Worse still, interest and central charges added a further £49 million to the deficit.

The report made the startling revelation that except for a tiny profit on hauling coal traffic none of the main classes of traffic covered their full costs. In terms of our focus on branch and minor lines the report was damning: 'Stopping trains are by far the worst loss maker. These trains, which derive little advantage from the speed of rail movement, are known to be very lightly loaded and to run, very largely, on routes which carry little traffic of any kind. Against direct costs alone they show losses almost equal to total receipts, and the overall loss is nearly twice that of receipts. On the other hand fast and semi-fast services, provided by through trains which mostly load well and operate over the routes with high traffic levels, show a substantial margin of receipts over direct costs, even though the group as a whole falls short of paying its full share of the system cost.'

Turning to freight the report confirmed that the disparity between the classes of traffic was just as great. Wagonload general merchandise, which loaded badly and gave rise to very little through train movement, was a bad loss-maker. The income from this source of traffic was £65 million but the direct costs associated with it were £97 million! Sundries traffic was bad for the same reason, the figures being income £38 million with direct costs of £52 million. The two categories of freight traffic that showed the best margin over direct costs were minerals and coal. As mentioned earlier, coal gave a small margin of profit over full cost, while mineral traffic fell just short of doing so. Apparently, it was difficult to analyse some traffic groups because descriptions and inclusions were somewhat arbitrary; however, some very interesting statistics appeared in the report, some of which appear below but not in a repetitious tabular form.

In 1961, following the closures in the preceding years, there were 17,830 route miles of track and a total track mileage of 34,150. As regards single track there were 5,900 route miles, 2,700 of which was freight only. The annual cost of maintaining a single track, depending on specification, was between £4,000 per mile for main lines and £2,000 per mile for the 3,500 miles falling within the lowest category of maintenance. The report pointed out that total track costs of £110 million excluded the costs associated with sidings, yards, stations and depots and yet it was almost one-quarter of the total annual receipts. Track costs were largely fixed and to cover costs even a single track route would need to carry high traffic densities. In addition to direct costs every class of both passenger and freight traffic also had a proportion of £168 million of indirect costs piled into the profit/loss equation.

Much of the report was based on a comprehensive traffic survey that was conducted during a single week, that ending 23 April 1961. The timing and method of this sample data gathering was a source of massive protest during public meetings, which in some cases took place between closure announcement and actual line closure. There were a number of inconsistencies and reports of evaluators counting passengers on the most lightly loaded train of the day, at the wrong time of day, and the wrong day of the week. Locals pointed to summer versus winter loadings and other peaks and troughs in traffic, but the report dealt with such variations in their narrative. 'The traffic surveys, which were made in great detail, extended over only one week, the week ending on 23rd April 1961, because it was impossible to continue the massive recording effort involved for a longer period. It was realised, therefore, that conclusions about some streams of traffic and about some parts of the system which are affected by seasonal changes could not be based firmly on the traffic surveys alone. Subject to this limitation, however, there can be little doubt about the general reliability of the picture revealed.' The dramatic conclusion was that 33 per cent of BR's total route miles carried only 1 per cent of the total passenger miles! Similarly one-third of the route miles carried only 1 per cent of the freight ton miles on BR. In broad brush terms the income from both passenger and freight traffic on all branch and minor lines was in excess of £4 million while the total costs of running the services was £20 million. Thus a £1 fare on a branch line was costing the railways £5, with £4 coming from either other business sectors or the taxpayer!

Including the figures detailed above the report confirmed that 50 per cent of BR's total route mileage carried only 4 per cent of passengers and 5 per cent of freight, total income from all sources on these routes being £20 million against costs of £40 million. By contrast, the other 50 per cent of the network covered its route costs by more than six times. The report recognised that these figures did not take account of the actual nature of the traffic on lightly loaded lines or the contributory value that they had to the remainder of the system but described any contribution as marginal at best and possibly negative.

◀ The station of Wolferton in Norfolk had a justifiable claim to fame in that it was in many respects a 'Royal' station, being situated on the edge of Her Majesty's Sandringham estate. The station was on the King's Lynn to Hunstanton branch line that opened in 1862 and over the years it hosted hundreds of royal trains. The ornate station, which even included crowns on top of the lamp standards, was extravagantly rebuilt in 1898. Despite its royal status the branch closed in May 1969. There were, however, no royal connections on this day as your humble author reboarded the King's Lynn-bound Metro-Cammell DMU in July 1968. *Author*

◀ In 1901, the population of St Ives in Cornwall was more than twice the size of St Ives in Huntingdonshire. However, the smaller town was once a junction for four routes, rather than being at the end of the single line branch of its contemporary. In years past the public could travel from St Ives to Huntingdon, March, Ely or Cambridge, but that all ended in October 1970 when the last of these lines, to Cambridge, closed to passengers. Sand trains continued to run to Fen Drayton and here, 8L43 headed by Class 37 No 6746 (No 37046) is seen at St Ives Junction in April 1970. Millions of pounds have been spent on a public 'guided busway' along the route (and on to Huntingdon), but at the time of writing it has still not opened, being over time and over budget. Right-minded people have been asking why they did not simply relay and reopen the railway line. *Author*

▼ With lines throughout East Anglia closing with increasing frequency there was a sense of urgency in travelling and photographing trains on doomed lines. For those journeying some distance the only chance of a photograph was to jump off the train they were travelling on, with the indulgence of the train crew, grab a photograph and rejoin the train. This resulted in a number of 'end of platform' shots, which have only become interesting in the fullness of time. Here, a March to King's Lynn via Wisbech train pauses at Smeeth Road in 1968, the line closing in September of that year. *Author*

▶ One of the joys of travelling along the old branch lines was spotting interesting items of infrastructure, some of which carried considerable age. With its gas mantles in situ this wonderful tapered gas lamp was operational at Swaffham in Norfolk on the King's Lynn to East Dereham line on the last day of service, 7 September 1968. Many such relics were sold to enthusiasts via Collector's Corner at Euston, or via local auctions. *Author*

▼ It was all very well for the local Consultative Committees to consider objections to closure and to consider arising hardship, but the process was something of a sham, at least from an individual perspective. It was highly unlikely that a closure decision would ever be reversed because, for example, this gentleman in the cloth cap would not be able to join this Dereham to King's Lynn service the following Monday in order to get to work. The scene is Swaffham, formerly the junction for Thetford, on the last day of service, 7 September 1968, with a green Metropolitan Cammell unit about to depart. *Author*

◄ This image is an amateur snap rather than a semi-professional photograph, but it shows a charming scene at Dunmere Halt on the Bodmin North to Boscarne Junction branch that opened as long ago as 1834, and was the first steam-hauled standard-gauge line in Cornwall. After steam had finished and under the control of BR(W), the primary service from Wadebridge to Bodmin was to Bodmin General, the former GWR station, with a feeder shuttle to and from Bodmin North, connecting at Boscarne Junction. The shuttle comprised a small, four-wheeled railbus and the green peril is seen passing Dunmere Halt in July 1966 with a train from Bodmin North. Despite this money-saving arrangement both lines closed to passengers in January 1967. Note that the train crew has failed to put the tail lamp on the back of the unit following the previous working. *Author's collection*

As regards stations the picture was similar with 33 per cent of a population of 7,000 stations producing only 1 per cent of total passenger receipts and 50 per cent producing only 2 per cent in total. At the other end of the scale less than 1 per cent of the stations produced 26 per cent of receipts. A broadly similar picture related to freight receipts. In terms of both lines and stations the report did not hold its punches and stated: 'There can be no question, therefore, that the railways would be better off financially if a high proportion of the stations were closed, even if this resulted in a total loss of traffic passing through them.'

The reshaping report went on to examine the various types of passenger train and here, we look at only the 'stopping train service', which excluded suburban services, but obviously included all branch lines, which were not identified specifically, although implied. In setting the scene the Beeching reshaping report said that as a group, stopping trains served the more rural communities by linking small towns and villages with each other and, sometimes rather indirectly, with one or more major towns. The report gave some background, pointing out that railway stopping services developed as the predominant form of rural public transport service in the 19th century, when the availability of private transport of any kind was very limited and the only alternative to the train were, where available, horse-drawn vehicles. Despite being at a fairly high cost per mile fare, even for third class, many of these services failed to pay their way.

◄ As already mentioned, a total of 22 four-wheeled railbuses were built in the late 1950s and they were deployed on lightly used routes to minimise running costs. The line from Kemble to Tetbury was the recipient of one of the tiny machines and in green livery with whiskers, such a unit is seen here at the Tetbury terminus. However, despite best efforts the line closed completely in April 1964 and was consigned to history. The line had opened in 1889 and to commemorate the event a plaque has been erected at the site of the demolished station. In addition the old goods shed has survived. *R.K. Blencowe collection*

▶ Far removed from either Cornwall or Gloucestershire is the Crieff branch in Scotland. A very well patronised Park Royal diesel railbus, No Sc79973, was photographed about one mile north of Gleneagles with the 3.17pm to Crieff on 4 July 1964. This was to be the last day of service on this Perthshire branch. The nine-mile line had its pre-Grouping origins with the Caledonian Railway. Intermediate stations were at Tullibardine, Muthill and Highlandman. *Michael Mensing*

It went on to point out that rail stopping services and bus services now served the same basic purpose, buses carrying the greater part of passengers moving by public transport in rural areas, and, as well as competing with each other, both forms of public transport were fighting a losing battle against private transport (the motor car). Immediately prior to the Second World War, in 1938, there were nearly 2 million private cars registered, but by 1954 there were over 3 million and it was predicted that by 1970 there would be 13 million. In addition there were nearly 2 million motorcycles. (There are now over 35 million vehicles registered in the UK.) Statistically the ownership rate of motor vehicles in rural areas was the same as in towns. It was estimated that branch trains catered for less than 10 per cent of rural transport needs and that on the whole, trains lost at least twice as much as they collected in fares.

An interesting statistic was that given a similar frequency of branch line service that a steam locomotive-hauled train cost between 2.5 and 3.5 times more to run than a diesel multiple unit. The report concluded that even where relatively low-cost diesel multiple units were running there would still be losses up to quite high levels of traffic. The report showed, based on certain criteria, that even where there was freight traffic capable of absorbing a share of the route cost, stopping passenger services (including branch lines) could not be regarded as paying their full cost below a passenger density of about 10,000 per week. To cover just movement costs would require 6,000 passengers per week. Where there was no other rail traffic, routes carrying up to 17,000 passengers per week would barely pay their way. Based on a six-day week and with a freight service this would mean that a branch line would require 1,666 passengers per day, or more than 200 passengers on every train, based on an eight-train per day service! Very few

branch lines could meet loading levels on that scale. Based on these figures the report concluded that money would be saved by discontinuing such services. It was also pointed out that a number of stopping services operating on more densely loaded routes were just as unsound financially because signalling had to be more complicated and small stations needed to be manned. A break-even figure of 10,000 passengers per week was placed on such services.

Out of the huge number of proposed closures the report detailed statistics pertaining to just three lines to demonstrate that their costings and therefore conclusions were justified. In the case of the Gleneagles to Crieff and Comrie branch in Scotland, ten trains per weekday operated over 15 miles with a modicum of seasonal traffic. On average there were five passengers on a train at any one time producing annual revenues of £1,900, a mere quarter of the £7,500 running expenses. If station terminal expenses of £3,500 and track and signalling costs of £8,200 were included then costs were ten times as much as earnings. However, passengers on the line contributed £12,000 to the earnings of other rail services, 75 per cent of which would be lost if the line closed. The annual net savings on closure were estimated at £8,400 (over £150,000 at current values).

It was a similar story on the Thetford to Swaffham line in Norfolk where there were on average nine passengers on each of the five trains per day each way, with annual earnings totalling £3,700 against total costs of £30,600. The gross revenue accruing to other services was £16,000, but the overall conclusion was that £29,000 (over £0.5 million at 2011 prices) would be saved annually by closure. Finally on an apparently better-used but much longer route from York to Beverley and on to Hull, a distance of 42 miles, there were an average of 57 passengers on each

▶ Closure protests were not all confined to written objections and public meetings and throughout the so-called 'Beeching era' there were a number of public protests. In this view at Ashford station in Kent on 4 October 1969, 17 members of the public protest against the proposition to close the line to Hastings. The New Romney branch had already closed and in 1969 the Minister of Transport had given approval for the closure of the route between Ashford and Ore, depriving the Romney Marsh area of any train service. They were successful, and the line remains open. Note the 'No more bloomers Marsh' sign, Sir Richard Marsh then being the Minister of Transport. *Author*

◀ This is one of the few photographs in this volume that has previously been published, albeit 35 years ago, but who could resist this heartfelt message from the station staff at Lyme Regis. The author visited the Lyme Regis branch exactly one week before closure and was greeted by this sign. The words were very profound and few would realise the ramifications of total closure of their local railway service. Whatever the circumstances, the line did close on 27 November 1965, and yet another delightful branch bit the dust. *Author*

train, which by that date was operated by diesel multiple units. Earnings of £90,400 covered operating expenses of £84,400 but when the other overheads were included in the calculations, such as station, track and signalling costs, the line allegedly lost over £60,400, equivalent to two-fifths of total direct expenses. Contributions to other rail services were complicated by there being an alternative route between Hull and York.

The reshaping report anticipated some of the more likely questions that might be posed by members of the public or other objectors to the report's conclusions. They anticipated that people would ask: Why not decrease fares and attract more traffic? Why not give people the opportunity to pay higher fares and preserve the service? Why not substitute rail buses for trains and decrease the cost of the service? Why not run fewer trains? Why not close some of the stations? The report somewhat patronisingly suggested that these were all common sense questions but that all experience showed that the problem could not be solved either by decreasing or increasing fares. However, it did not deal with the questions lightly and spent some space explaining the rationale.

The report explained that if fares were halved, traffic would have to increase at least fourfold to cover the direct costs of stopping services as a group (it would have been impossible to have provided detailed costings of every branch line in the main report) and six-fold to make them pay their whole cost. Nobody could seriously hope that this would happen. People without their own transport were not so seriously deterred by the rail fares for short journeys that they would use trains many times as often if fares were halved. To cover the costs of many services fares would have to be increased by eight or ten times their then current levels even if traffic remained at its present density. Most traffic would of course disappear completely at those fare levels. The replacement of trains by railbuses ignored the cost of providing the route itself and also ignored that railbuses were more expensive vehicles than road buses. It would still be necessary to have (again on average) a passenger density of 14,000 per week, to cover the cost of the total service, as compared with 17,000 for a diesel multiple unit. In other words, the operational savings of a railbus over a DMU was less than 17 per cent.

Similarly, a thinning out of the stations or a reduction in services would not make a service self-supporting even if it had no adverse effect on revenue. Overall it was folly to believe that stopping services could be preserved, as an economic alternative to buses or private transport, even if some ingenuity was shown by the railway operators. Consequently, a high proportion of stopping passenger train services ought to be discontinued as soon as possible, and that many of the lightly loaded lines over which they operated should close as well, unless they carried exceptional freight traffic. All stopping (and branch) services had been examined individually, and so had all lengths of lightly loaded route.

There followed a rather stark recommendation that there could be no doubt about the desirability of closing those services that did not meet the financial tests and it was the wish of the railways to close them as soon as the procedures permitted. Questions of hardship would be considered by the Transport Users Consultative Committee (TUCC). There followed a lengthy seven-page tabulation by way of Appendix, of the lines to be closed, followed by a 20-page double column list of stations recommended for closure. This part of the report was to be a bombshell for thousands of railwaymen and much of the rural (and not so rural) population. A total of about 5,000 route miles were recommended for closure and some 2,000 stations and halts. A warning was given that once the hopelessly uneconomic lines had been dealt with the remaining stopping services would be reviewed and should they be found to be uneconomic they would be similarly dealt with, resulting in another round of closures.

Dr Beeching shunted the responsibility for hardship issues to the TUCC, which to be fair, was the process included in the Transport Act 1962. He admitted that it would be folly to suggest that the widespread closure of stopping train services would cause no hardship anywhere or to anybody. For the judgement of the closure proposals as a whole, it would be necessary to have some idea of the scale and degree of hardship that they were likely to cause. In a broad overstatement the report stated that except for northern Scotland and parts of central Wales most areas of the country were already served by a network of bus services, more dense than the network of rail services to be withdrawn, and in the majority of cases buses already carried the major proportion of local traffic. With some minor exceptions these buses catered for the same traffic flows as the railways, on routes that were largely parallel. Taken as a whole they had enough spare capacity to absorb the traffic that would be displaced from the railways, which would do no more than replace the bus traffic that had been lost over the past decade, and which would provide a welcome addition to the revenue of the bus operators. In all of these cases a need for special services would be rare but there may be localities where there was not already a bus service connecting places served by rail (try telling that to a would-be passenger from Blandford Forum to Radstock!).

It was estimated that only 122 miles (out of 5,000 miles!) of the routes for closure were not already paralleled by a bus service. It appeared therefore that in most areas of the country hardship would arise only on a very limited scale. Although the report contained both accurate information and spurious figures the last sentence must have been a statement that was a distortion of the truth, possibly to sooth any anguish in the corridors of power.

So far we have looked at the Beeching reshaping plan in terms of passenger services but more of the report was given over to the subject of freight, operating and administration, and manpower. In those wonderful nostalgic images from times past mail sacks would appear from the local branch passenger train and parcels for several local trades people would be placed on the platform for local delivery, while in the goods yard a few tons of coal, a few sacks of fertiliser and maybe a few planks of building timber would be unloaded from a couple of wagons left by the daily goods train. The pick-up goods would be formed along the line collecting wagons for onward transmission to a distant marshalling yard. By the time of the *Reshaping of British Railways* report this nationwide wagonload traffic had become hopelessly uneconomic. The obligation to be a 'common carrier' meant that few freight loads could be refused by the railway and the charges did not reflect the true cost of conveying the various commodities. Consequently this type of traffic was bound to receive scathing criticisms from Dr Beeching, and the report did not disappoint.

Slightly outside the general freight category was mail and parcels, handled on behalf of the Post Office. Schedules of services were agreed with the Post Office for the conveyance of mails seven days per week. The majority of letter mails were carried by rail either on normal passenger trains or by dedicated letter-sorting vehicles travelling overnight. Letter mails were loaded into and unloaded from train vans by Post Office staff, and were transferred by them at intermediate stations if necessary. Post Office parcels were mainly carried on passenger trains but were loaded and unloaded by railway staff. In addition, the railway itself accepted, collected and delivered parcels for carriage by passenger trains, or by booked special parcels trains, during normal business hours on six days of the week. A countrywide service was available to and from all stations open to passengers, and also (surprisingly) to some stations which were formerly served by passenger trains. No extra charge was made for collection and delivery, other than in exceptional circumstances.

The report stated that the withdrawal of stopping services (including branch lines) would reduce the number of places where parcels could be handled, but that no great volume of traffic would be affected. The Post Office was charged with resolving any problems that would arise. There was considerable overlapping of the Post Office and British Railways parcels systems, which lost both organisations money. The Post Office delivered parcels but did not collect them from individuals, except if at their convenience. The railways collected and delivered parcels of any shape and size up to 2cwt (224lb). In 1961, the railways handled 50 million bags of parcels for the Post Office containing 255 million parcels with an average weight of 5lb and a take of £30 million, £12 million of which went into the coffers of the railway. The railways conveyed 84 million parcels within their own system with net receipts of £27 million (some £500 million in 2011 values). The traffic patterns were similar to passenger and freight receipts, in this case 3,386 smaller stations handling only 4 per cent of the parcels while the largest 22 stations handled 45 per cent. The Post Office

lost over £8 million on their parcels service and the railways revenue made an inadequate contribution to system costs. Both were in competition with road transport, particularly British Road Services. It was reported that discussions would take place to see whether there was scope for amalgamation, thereby eliminating duplication of effort and resources as well as considering better means of handling the traffic.

In terms of freight traffic a lengthy introduction outlining the history of the movement of freight by rail was included. It was explained that the railways were developed to the fullest extent when the horse and cart was the only means of transporting goods to and from the railheads. This resulted in branches and sidings spawning in large numbers because of the difficulty in conveying merchandise more than a few miles. Combined with station sidings the method of operation resulted in many single wagonload consignments. As a consequence the railway wagon became the primary unit of movement. Instead of becoming part of a through freight train, nearly all goods moved by the staging of wagons from marshalling yard to marshalling yard, with variable and cumulative delays at each stage, resulting in a slow and unpredictable journey. Hence the railways saddled themselves with the costly movement of wagons in small numbers over a multiplicity of branch lines, where there were too few wagons moving to make up economically viable goods trains. At the same time the railways sacrificed the speed, reliability, and low cost of through train operation even on the main arteries. The report went on to make a very relevant point that had been a major obstacle to progress.

The slow and semi-random movement of wagons, and their dispersal over many small terminals where they could not be collected or delivered frequently, had necessitated the provision of an enormous fleet of wagons. Also, because of their random motion, all of these wagons had to be capable of coupling and running with one another and going almost anywhere on the system. This compatibility requirement, combined with the size and the cost of the fleet, had been a great obstacle to technical progress, since the new always has to mate with the old. In consequence, evolution of improved rolling stock had been very slow.

In later years the problem was compounded by BR handling wagons with no brakes, manual brakes, vacuum brakes and air brakes. Performance figures were appalling with an average turn-round time between loading and unloading for British Railways wagons of nearly 12 days. The wagons were in transit for between 1½ and 2 days, although the average wagon journey length was just 67 miles! The report did not pull its punches and described the slow and variable delivery times as 'quite unacceptable', especially as road transport easily made such journeys in a single day. Beeching said that transition was not possible and there needed to be a complete break with the past by developing new services with new rolling stock not

▲ The old 'Slow and Dirty' alias the Somerset & Dorset Joint railway had a special place in the hearts of railway enthusiasts. The author was fortunate enough to travel the route several times during 1965/66. The line had been immortalised by the camera of the late Ivo Peters who chased trains between Bath and Bournemouth in his Bentley car, in the days when the UK had a robust manufacturing industry. In this evocative scene the Highbridge branch train leaves Templecombe Upper behind Ivatt 2-6-2T No 41283 on 27 September 1965, while No 41296 stands by. The main network closed in March 1966. *Author*

▼ It seems hard to believe that a town the size of Devizes in Wiltshire, with a population of about 30,000, cannot support a railway service. However, Devizes has now been without trains for 45 years and residents have to travel to either Melksham, some 6.8 miles distant, or Pewsey, 9.7 miles away, to catch a train. In this 1964 view a green-liveried DMU is seen at the substantial station with a train for Newbury. The line between Holt Junction and Patney and Churton via Devizes closed from 18 April 1966, the Holt section having been built and opened by the Wiltshire, Somerset & Weymouth Railway back in 1857. *E.T. Gill*

◄ This extreme rarity shows one of the 1,700hp Beyer Peacock 'Hymek' diesel-hydraulics at Portishead on 28 October 1964. No D7023 is about to depart for Bristol Temple Meads and during its journey it will pass under the Clifton Suspension Bridge on the banks of the River Avon. The branch closed to passengers in September 1964 but freight traffic continued until December 1983. The branch is a potential candidate for reinstatement, subject to finance being available, which in the present climate seems highly unlikely. *E.T. Gill*

◄ The GWR branch line between Taunton and Barnstaple was a lengthy line that skirted the southern fringe of the Exmoor National Park. The entire 45¾-mile line closed to all traffic from 3 October 1966, the connecting Exe Valley line from Exeter to Dulverton having closed previously, in October 1963. When photographed the Dulverton station running-in board seems to have had the legend 'Change for Exe Valley Line' deleted. Dulverton station was nearly two miles from the town it served. A two-car DMU with small yellow warning panel on its way from Barnstaple Junction to Taunton pauses on the last day of service. *Author*

◄ What could be better than a trundle down the Culm Valley Light Railway in the brakevan of the daily milk train? Armed with permits and having paid a token fare, the author and two colleagues organised a ride behind North British Class 22 No D6333 on 12 September 1970. The train pauses on its way to Hemyock for the guard to close the crossing gates at Uffculme. Passenger trains had ceased in September 1963, but milk traffic would continue for a further 12 years. The track alignment was severed by the M5 motorway just east of Tiverton Junction station. *Author*

compatible with the old, which would progressively displace the common-user wagon fleet and the system of operation which employed it.

The main classes of freight traffic were coal, coke and solid fuels, mineral traffic such as iron ore, limestone, china clay, steel, fertiliser etc. and general merchandise, covering a wide range of commodities. Of these only coal traffic was profitable and that only marginally. Wagonload traffic under the general merchandise label was financially disastrous losing, with sundry traffic, over £75 million (£1.3 billion today!). Another potential problem was the inability of the railways to increase the volume of coal carried as they were largely in the hands of the power generating companies and if anything, domestic coal consumption was set to reduce and the ton/miles figure would fall. Also, large numbers of collieries did not have the equipment for rapid and efficient loading. The report accurately predicted the evolution of the merry-go-round system using larger, high-capacity, fully braked, hopper wagons that could be hauled at higher speeds and loaded/unloaded quickly. Any likely increase in minerals traffic was considered to be marginal, which left only general merchandise as an area of growth, but that was the greatest loss-maker.

Shocking waste and inefficiency was identified in the report. For example, there were 5,031 stations open to coal traffic in 1960. Although open to receive coal, 1,172 stations received no coal consignments whatsoever. A further 1,790 stations received only between one and five wagons per week. At the other end of the scale the 64 largest stations received over 50,000 tons each, while just over 2,000 stations received between 2,500 and 50,000 tons per year. The report argued that only a 'few hundred' properly equipped depots were required, capable of receiving through or dedicated trains. Some such concentration depots had been opened. Minerals traffic did benefit from running block trains and few recommendations were made. The same could not be said for general merchandise, which included an immense variety of goods and commodities. A survey of all freight traffic was undertaken in the same week as the survey on passenger levels. The traffic surveyed during this week amounted to 1.7 million tons. It was determined what proportion of traffic flowed between terminals of different kinds, how each of these groups was spread over different ranges of distances moved, how they varied in wagon loading, and how the costs of the various groups compared with receipts. The conclusion was that wagonload freight was a bad loss-maker when taken as a group. However, over half of the traffic was siding to siding, much of which moved in trainload quantities, and this made a good contribution to system costs. One-third of the remainder moved between sidings and docks, and this fell just short of covering its direct costs. The remaining 30 per cent of the whole passed through stations, at one or both ends of its transit, and caused losses that were so large that they extinguished any surpluses that were made on all the rest.

Freight sundries that were classified under general merchandise were also a bad loss-maker with poor wagon loadings and high levels of transshipment. Of a 950-station total some 700, or 73 per cent, handled less than 25 tons of merchandise per day. It was recommended that BR select only the flows that were most suitable for rail movement and that the number of depots handling such commodities should be reduced to 100, to be mainly located in large towns and cities. Beeching realised that the way forward in many areas would be 'liner trains' and containers were also given a positive mention. The only other areas affecting branch and minor lines were reductions in manpower, an obvious consequence of the vast number of line and station closures recommended. Overall it was proposed to eliminate 70,000 jobs over a three-year period.

There is no doubt that although the reshaping report contained a wealth of detail showing many areas of BR operation that were hopeless loss-makers, it was the tabulations of line and station closures that hit the headlines and shocked the public, resulting in the report and Dr Richard Beeching becoming infamous.

In branch line terms the 1960s and the so-called 'Beeching era' would see the demise of hundreds of railway lines, too numerous to mention individually but covering all areas of the BR network. The public hearings were something of a farce. Posters giving notice of closure were posted, objections went to the TUCC, meetings were held where the public were not allowed to challenge BR facts and figures, or determine precisely which overheads had been included in loss-making calculations, or how much credit had been given for through ticketing etc. On rare occasions closure decisions were overridden by the Central TUCC but even in these circumstances the Minister of Transport had a final veto. Finally, after the last rites were given on the last day of service, as previously described, lines did close. Some closed completely while others had passenger services withdrawn but remained open for freight. Many of these survivors also closed, often within a relatively short period of time, for example the Helston branch in Cornwall.

Happily a handful of branches remained open because of awkward terrain and difficulties in securing bus replacements, such as the Gunnislake branch in Cornwall, although it was cut back from the original terminus at Callington. Others had very heavy traffic in the summer months, such as the Looe and St Ives branches in Cornwall, while the nearby branches to Helston, Fowey and Bodmin all closed. Some lines survived and boomed, for example Witham to Braintree and Bocking and the Southminster branch, which were both electrified, while the neighbouring branch from Witham to Maldon did close.

Some branches held on by a thread for over ten years, such as that to Bridport in Dorset, while several others, for example the Exmouth branch, Darlington to Bishop Auckland, Barrow to Whitehaven, Ashford to Hastings,

Inverness to Wick, York to Harrogate, and the Blaenau Ffestiniog branch, all cheated death entirely. However, overall a significant percentage of the lines and stations identified for closure in the reshaping report did close, in their hundreds. Some of the closures gave preservationists the chance to acquire redundant branch lines outright and nearly half a century later many are thriving, although noticeably few offer a daily commuter service, possibly because Beeching was right?

There is no disguising the fact, however, that the Beeching report, later referred to as the 'Beeching axe', had a profound effect on the nation's railways. Over 5,000 route miles of railway line and 2,363 stations were closed. In 1950, the BR network comprised 21,000 route miles of railway line and 6,000 stations, but by 1975, after full Beeching report implementation, there were just 12,000 route miles and approximately 2,000 stations. Only one in three of the rail passengers ever transferred to the replacement buses. Towards the end of the decade the 1968 Transport Act was passed and for the first time it was recognised that there was such a thing as a 'social railway' that provided a public service, which should be subsidised in certain circumstances. The great irony of the Beeching years was that despite all of the closures and economies the central overheads were not substantially reduced and BR continued to run at a loss (as railways tend to in the majority of countries). There is no doubt that many loss-making branch line services should have been withdrawn but due to demographic changes and population growth many of the more marginal closures would probably now be profitable, as well as making a contribution to environmental issues.

Before Dr Beeching departed from his BR post in 1965 and returned to ICI he oversaw the production of another report, *The Development of Major Trunk Routes* sometimes called 'Beeching 2', which identified routes deemed worthy of further large-scale expenditure. He considered that there was still far too much duplication of trunk routes and that of a total of 7,500 miles just over 3,000 should be further developed. As the report did not impact branches or minor lines it is worth no more than a passing mention here. There is no doubt that the 1960s decade was the most poignant, indeed the most dramatic, in the history and decline of the British branch line. For his efforts the good doctor was to become Lord Beeching and his memory will be guaranteed by road names throughout the country, such as 'Beeching Close', 'Beeching Way' and 'Beeching Drive' (see page 7).

▼ In days gone by the Midland Railway, North Staffordshire Railway and LNWR all had a presence in the Burton upon Trent area, which rightly or wrongly was, in national terms, best known for its breweries. One of the local passenger services that survived until 13 June 1960 ran between Burton and Tutbury, which was latterly operated by push-pull steam trains. Propelling its coaches at Stretton & Clay Mills is Ivatt 2MT No 41277 with the 4.37pm Tutbury to Burton upon Trent on 4 June 1960. *Michael Mensing*

▲ To those who visited Highbridge towards the end of branch line services from Evercreech Junction, which ceased in March 1966, it seemed inconceivable that signs would point the way to seven platforms, especially as only two were used for trains on the Bristol to Taunton main line. However, the old Somerset & Dorset Railway once had a major works and depot at Highbridge and even in 1965, as one branch train arrived another was ready to depart for Evercreech. Ivatt 2-6-2T No 41290 has just arrived in charge of a utility parcels van and a single coach. The line between the signalboxes gave access to the main line and the Burnham-on-Sea branch (see page 55). *Author*

▼ The versatile Ivatt 2-6-2Ts were numbered within the London Midland Region 40000 to 59999 range, but gradually they replaced older classes of steam locomotive on other regions, especially the Southern and Western Regions. Putting in a sprightly performance with the 9.08am from Guildford, Surrey, No 41294 and its three coaches are seen between Bramley and Cranleigh on a delightful 20 May 1965. All services ceased just three weeks later and the track between Guildford (Peasmarsh Junction) and Christ's Hospital would soon be lifted, the line failing to celebrate its centenary by less than four months. *Author*

▲ Although the Longmoor Military Railway was not a BR branch line it eventually connected the branch terminus of Bordon with Liss on the Portsmouth Direct main line. A series of standard-gauge lines were ready for service between 1905 and 1907 and the railway was used by Royal Engineers to train military personnel in railway operations, which they practised throughout the world. There were many sidings to various depots and also a 'Hollywater loop' that allowed continuous running. Members of the public and servicemen were carried on the branch service from Liss to Longmoor and here, an old 'birdcage' coach and LMR 0-6-0ST No 196 are seen at the former location. The entire operation closed in 1971 and an attempt to preserve part of the line was thwarted by local residents. *Author*

◄ This well-composed shot features the branch goods at Coldstream in Berwickshire on the old North Eastern Railway line from Tweedmouth, south of Berwick-upon-Tweed, to Kelso and St Boswells. Opened as Cornhill in 1849, the station was renamed Coldstream in 1873. What was curious was the fact that the town is in Scotland but the railway station was across the River Tweed in England! The line closed to passengers in June 1964 and to goods in March 1965, ending scenes such as this with 2MT 2-6-0 No 46482 indulging in a shunting movement on 1 June 1962. *Michael Mensing*

▲ This illustrates a part of the BR network that was very rarely photographed, the now-closed freight lines to the east of Whitehaven. These lines ran from Sellafield through Egremont to Cleator Moor and Rowrah, and down to Whitehaven, originally part of the Whitehaven, Cleator & Egremont Joint Railway (run by the Furness Railway and the LNWR). Passing the closed Wood End station with a northbound brakevan on 25 June 1968 is 'Clayton' Class 17 No D8502. These unsuccessful locomotives had a short lifespan, some lasting only six years in service. *Michael Mensing*

▼ Although holiday traffic continued to visit the Lincolnshire seaside town of Mablethorpe in the summer months throughout the late 1960s, for the majority of the year loadings on the branch from Willoughby were light. In fact the line north of Mablethorpe through Saltfleetby to Louth had closed to passengers from 5 December 1960. Inevitably the remaining line was included on the closure list and it duly succumbed in October 1970. The four-platform station supported a W.H. Smith kiosk, which appears to be selling beach balls and postcards to visitors. *Author*

▲ London Docklands has changed enormously over the past 40 years where all the old-fashioned shipping practices have been overtaken by global containerisation. The rapid death of the London Docks required regeneration and although it took some time to truly 'take off', few would have anticipated the massive skyscrapers and luxury apartments that we see today. With ships and dockside cranes in the background, 'Toffee Apple' Class 33/0 No D5513 (later No 31013) arrives at North Woolwich with the 3.28pm from Stratford (Low Level) on 1 October 1962. The line was electrified in 1985 but was caught up with future transport strategy, the route being part duplicated by a Docklands Light Railway extension. The line closed on 9 December 2006. *Author's collection*

▼ This photograph illustrates a complex working at Kidsgrove, featuring a phenomenon now virtually eliminated, the 'workman's train'. The 4.26pm departure from Crewe was empty coaching stock destined for the Royal Ordnance Factory staff at Radway Green, near Alsagar. The train would take the loop line via Burslem at Kidsgrove (Liverpool Road) having left the Crewe line, reverse onto the Macclesfield line and reverse again on its way to Stoke-on-Trent. The power provided on 26 September 1960 was Stanier 2-6-4T No 42668. *Michael Mensing*

▲ Even in the heady days before the Second World War there were only three trains per day in each direction on the little-known 13-mile branch line between Montrose and Inverbervie, a small town with just over 1,000 inhabitants. Passenger services had their last gasp in October 1951 but goods trains continued to trundle their way along the line until May 1966. Under the BR Reshaping Plan this is precisely the type of uneconomic working that in the view of Dr Beeching and his associates, needed to be eradicated. Descending into the long-closed Lauriston station with two box vans and a brake on 8 July 1964, this J37 class 0-6-0 No 64608 is running tender first on the run from Montrose. *Michael Mensing*

▼ Merchandise in barrels and a handcart date this photograph at the Scottish terminus station of Eyemouth at the end of the short branch from Burnmouth. On 15 June 1961, J39 class 0-6-0 No 64917 and its single maroon brake composite coach were photographed prior to their return to Burnmouth. The entire branch closed in February 1962. The advertisement on the side of the double-decker assures the public that they stand a chance of winning a fortune on Littlewood's football pools. *Gavin Morrison*

▲ Making the quantum leap from Berwickshire to Caithness we find Sulzer Type 2 Class 26 No 5332 (later No 26032) arriving at the outpost of Georgemas Junction, 715 rail miles from London, with a train from Wick. This working to Inverness will be joined to a two-coach portion from Thurso before continuing along the old Highland Railway route. These distant locations are still rail served and three trains per day make the 161½-mile journey in each direction, which even with today's modern high-performance units, takes nearly four hours. *Author*

▼ A visit to the Isle of Wight during the mid-1960s was always something to look forward to because it was tantamount to entering a time warp, at least as far as the railways were concerned. Period pre-Grouping coaches and modified Adams O2 class 0-4-4T steam locomotives were the mainstay of numerous routes. Passing the semaphore signals at Ryde Pier Head on 29 March 1965 is No 18 *Ningwood* with a train from Ventnor. In a little over 12 months this scene would be relegated to the annals of history when the line was electrified. *Author*

▲ Since 1952 the IoW network had been shrinking and from the end of April 1966 only the line from Ryde to Shanklin remained. The railways of the Isle of Wight needed modernising and after much head scratching to overcome problems associated with loading gauge clearances, an idea was generated to electrify the remaining line and to use old redundant London Underground stock. Although the line was closed for about three months during 1967, modernisation work had continued throughout 1966, including the addition of the third rail. On 21 December 1966, just ten days before steam ended, No 27 *Merstone* climbs towards Smallbrook Junction with the 11.30 from Ryde Pier Head. *Author*

▼ The line from Brockenhurst to Lymington opened in 1858 by the independent Lymington Railway. However, its claim to lasting fame came during 1967 when the line was said to be the last steam-hauled standard-gauge branch line on BR. Some disputed this, stating the honour fell to the Clapham Junction to Kensington Olympia service, although the latter was not a branch line in a classic sense. With the unmistakeable outline of a Bulleid coach in the foreground, BR Standard 2-6-4T No 80146 prepares to depart for Lymington Town and Brockenhurst in March 1967. *Author*

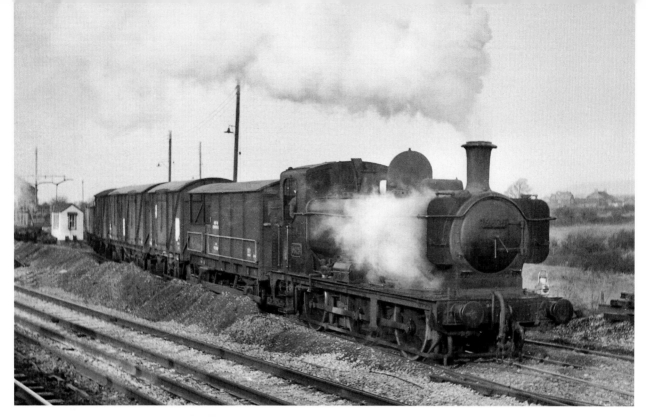

▲ One of the author's earliest South Wales steam shots shows 0-6-0PT No 9625 coming off the by then freight-only line from Cefn Junction at Pyle in January 1965. The line continued to carry goods until November 1973. Railway history in the Pyle area dates back to 1828 when a railway from Dyffryn Colliery to Porthcawl Harbour opened. Pyle was better known as the junction for the Porthcawl branch, which closed to passengers in September 1963. The GWR-style brakevan was 'not in common use'. *Author*

▼ It is not only in Lancashire and Yorkshire where factory chimney stacks can be seen in railway photographs. There are 14 stacks in the background as 0-6-0PT No 6434 and a single brake coach pass Darby End Halt in Staffordshire with the 7pm Old Hill to Dudley (Blowers Green) auto-train, on 14 May 1964. The line closed to passengers in June 1964 but continued in freight use until 1968. The station platforms can just be detected on the far left. *Michael Mensing*

▲ There are towns and villages named Fawley in Hampshire, Buckinghamshire, Berkshire and Herefordshire, but this view shows the latter on the Gloucester to Hereford via Grange Court and Ross-on-Wye line. At least a couple of passengers are waiting on the platform as a GWR large Prairie 2-6-2T, No 4161, runs through the passing loop and brakes for the stop with the 1.40pm Hereford to Gloucester train on 28 March 1964. The clock was ticking towards total closure, which occurred later in the year. *Michael Mensing*

▼ Last days of service produced some amazing scenes and evocative photographs as local folks turned out to wish their fond farewells to, what for many, had been a way of life for many decades. In this nostalgic scene at Doseley (Salop), on the Wellington to Much Wenlock branch, the very last train on the last day of service, Saturday 21 July 1962, is being celebrated. Well-wishers (or perhaps mourners) look on, a wreath has been applied to the smokebox door of polished 5101 class 2-6-2T No 4178, and a cynical headboard 'The Beeching Special' appears on the 7.05pm from Much Wenlock! Services were officially withdrawn from 23 July 1962, the Monday following the last day of service. The line beyond Much Wenlock to Craven Arms had been closed much earlier, in December 1951.
Michael Mensing

▲ Kingham (formerly Chipping Norton Junction) was a relatively busy place in railway crossroads terms. In addition to what were then main line trains running between London, Oxford, Worcester and Hereford, branch trains on the Cheltenham to Banbury via Chipping Norton route called at the station using connecting spurs. In addition, there were a few trains that started and ended their journeys at Kingham. In this study from 2 September 1961, 2-6-2T No 4142 departs with the 4pm to Chipping Norton. The sections of line to the latter point and to Cheltenham both closed in 1962, the line beyond Chipping Norton having closed to passengers in 1951. Unbelievably, in 1910, the 'branch' hosted a through Cardiff to Newcastle upon Tyne express! *Michael Mensing*

▼ The Bewdley branch line connection takes up most of the space on the running-in board at Woofferton Junction. The station was on the Welsh Marches (or 'North & West') line but it closed at the same time as the branch line to Tenbury Wells in July 1961, the 'junction' role being its only purpose. No 1445 is seen at the head of an auto-train that will shortly be heading off to Tenbury Wells on 29 July 1961, the last day of service. The line beyond to Bewdley closed the following year. *SLS*

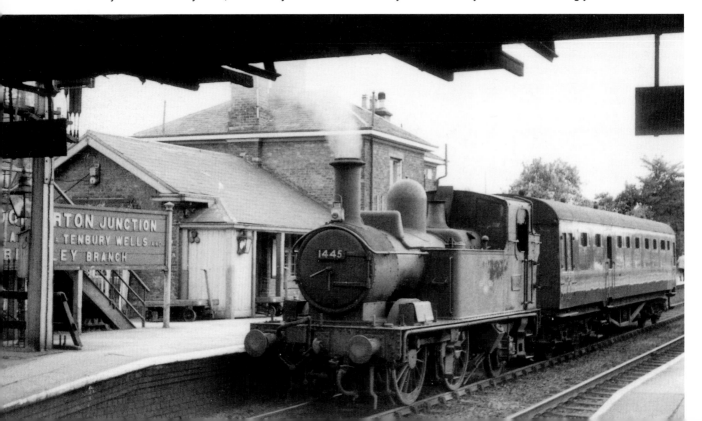

▲ The total area taken up by the two railway routes that ran through Lydford in Devon was considerable. For a short distance the GWR Plymouth (Tavistock Junction) to Launceston branch line ran parallel to the LSWR main line from Exeter and Okehampton to Plymouth. This view of the GWR station finds 4575 class 2-6-2T No 5569 taking water at the head of a Launceston to Plymouth working in July 1962. The service was withdrawn in December, just five months later. *W.A. Camwell*

▼ The long association of Beattie 0298 class 2-4-0 well tank locomotives with the Wadebridge to Wenford Bridge line was sufficient incentive for many railway photographers to seek out the ancient locomotives along the route of the Camel Valley. The first member of the class arrived on the line in May 1893 and the last of the class to depart Cornwall was in 1962, a tenure of 69 years. The class was originally introduced in 1874 but the locomotives were subsequently rebuilt on more than one occasion, yet without losing their charm. No 30585 is seen shunting china clay wagons at Boscarne Junction on 10 November 1961. *Donald Luscombe/SLS*

▲ On occasions branch lines closed due to flood damage or landslips and where the line was lightly used a decision had to be made whether the extent of the problem was beyond economic repair. One such casualty was the 56-mile Carmarthen to Aberystwyth line that closed between December 1964 and February 1965 due to flood damage near Strata Florida. On 1 August 1960, 'Manor' class 4-6-0 No 7803 *Barcote Manor* brings the 10.35am from Carmarthen into Aberystwyth. The Welsh seaside town was first rail connected in 1864, but via the Cambrian route. *Michael Mensing*

◄ The Looe branch in Cornwall was one of five survivors as other Cornish branches closed their doors for business. While Launceston, Callington (part), Bodmin General, Bodmin North, Padstow and the North Cornwall line, Bude, Fowey, Chacewater to Newquay and Helston all lost their passenger services, Gunnislake, Looe, Newquay, Falmouth and St Ives somehow survived. Here, a single power car stands at Looe in 1969, having arrived from Liskeard. The miserable shelter replaced a fine station building, but the former cost virtually nothing to maintain. *Author*

▶ One wonders how many people, other than the guard who is observing the photographer, were travelling on this Petersfield to Midhurst train on 10 September 1950, nearly five years before closure. The M7 class 0-4-4T, No 30047, would have an easy task toying with a single compartment coach. The train is leaving Rogate, one of two intermediate stations, the other being Elstead. The station was well over a mile from the village. *Author's collection*

▼ Dieselisation eventually came to surviving branches whether they remained in operation for passenger or freight services. By 1966 the goods service from Horsham and Pulborough to Petworth had been reduced to thrice weekly, as required. On 24 April 1966 the train was 'required' and an English Electric 350hp shunter is seen passing Fittleworth with some empty coal wagons. Note that the guard has a good fire going in his brakevan. The line would close completely four weeks later. *Author*

▲ Branch line photography, especially on freight-only lines, has never been easy and long waits are sometimes called for. Back in 1969 the aggregate train to Ardingly, Sussex, ran very early in the morning and an early start was necessary, and for much of the year the train ran in the dark. At 06.15 on 8 July 1969, Class 73 electro-diesel No E6029 (later No 73122) eases off the branch at Copyhold Junction, near Haywards Heath on the Brighton main line, with empty hoppers. The previously electrified line once continued through to Horsted Keynes. *Author*

▼ Another electro-diesel using its 600hp auxiliary diesel engine on a non-electrified branch line is No E6025 (later No 73119) seen beside the River Adur between Shoreham-by-Sea and the now-closed Beeding Cement Works, on 13 April 1971. The once double-track line ran through from the Coastway West line at Shoreham-by-Sea to the Mid-Sussex or Arun Valley line at Christ's Hospital, although service trains worked through from Brighton to Horsham. Goods trains to the cement works ceased during 1988, and the trackbed here is now a footpath. *Author*

▲ Ballachulish (Glencoe) station in the West Highlands, the terminus of a long, 27½-mile branch line from Connell Ferry, some six miles from Oban, had the most magnificent backdrop. The Caledonian Railway terminus building was set at right angles to the buffer stops. With some scorch marks at the bottom of the smokebox door Pickersgill CR 0-4-4T No 55238 is having its coal bunker attended to by the fireman before departure with the 3.57pm to Oban on 20 May 1960. There seems to be activity in the goods yard, where three box vans are visible. The entire line closed in March 1966. *Michael Mensing*

▼ A year later than the picture above, No 55263 was still at work on the Ballachulish branch but on this occasion was photographed enveloped in steam leaving the wooden platform of North Connell with the 10.48am from Ballachulish, on 18 May 1961. The distance from Oban to Ballachulish was less than 34 miles but the train took about 1½ hours for the journey. At the terminus there were booked bus connections for Kinlochleven. A note in Bradshaw's timetable warned passengers that 'all trains stop at Barcaldine Siding, when required, to pick up or set down passengers'! *Michael Mensing*

▲ The scene is Tongland on the Castle Douglas to Kirkcudbright (pronounced *Kerkoobree*) branch line at a point where both rail and road once crossed the River Dee, but now the car is king. Heading the 9.30am from Kirkudbright to the junction station at Castle Douglas is BR Standard 2-6-4T No 80023 on 11 July 1963. The branch line opened in 1864 and closed in May 1965 and just one month later the 'main' line from Dumfries to Challoch Junction, near Stranraer, also closed. Goods facilities were withdrawn from the branch at the same time. *Michael Mensing*

▼ The 1886 Killin Junction to Killin branch has already been featured but this photograph shows a curiosity on the line. Although the branch finally closed on 27 September 1965 the extension from Killin to Loch Tay had closed to passengers as long ago as 11 September 1939. However, the branch engine shed was located at Loch Tay and so the line remained open for light engine running between Killin and the shed. On 17 May 1961 0-4-4T No 55204 heads off through the weeds in a sylvan setting at Loch Tay towards Killin, its coal bunker having been amply replenished. *Michael Mensing*

▶ Nowadays Alton Towers is where weary parents take their children in an attempt to provide a day's entertainment, although one suspects that the adults enjoy many facilities as much as their offspring. However, when this photograph was taken on 19 August 1961 such activities did not exist and so the railway line could not benefit from what would have been a lucrative income. The town had a rather solid-looking North Staffordshire Railway station building and pausing on 19 August 1961 with the 11.25am Leek to Uttoxeter is Fowler 4MT 2-6-4T No 42323 with three maroon coaches in tow. Sadly, the line closed to passengers in January 1965. The Churnet Valley Railway has plans to extend its railway as far as Alton. The station survives and is now owned by the Landmark Trust. *Michael Mensing*

▼ There is an immense amount of detail in this photograph of Evesham (Midland) station dating back to 1962. In the background can be seen the GWR station on the still-open Cotswold Line between Oxford and Worcester. The MR/LMS station was on a route from Barnt Green and Redditch to Ashchurch. The line south of Redditch through to Ashchurch officially closed on 17 June 1963, but due to the poor condition of the track, substitute bus services had operated the service from 1 October 1962. With vintage railway infrastructure surrounding, this Fowler 4MT 2-6-4T, No 42416 (with cab side windows), departs for Redditch with the 4.30pm from Ashchurch on 14 April 1962. Some trains worked through to Birmingham New Street, the 43½-mile journey from Ashchurch taking some two hours to complete. *Michael Mensing*

▲ Various types of LMS 2-6-4Ts were widely used on branch line duties with well over 600 examples attributed to Fowler, Stanier and Fairburn. They were heavy beasts, each weighing between 85 and 92 tons and their capability was well beyond the two coaches seen here. With the number obscured by dirt and grime this example is seen near Padeswood with the 4.30pm Chester (General) to Denbigh on 28 April 1962, the very last day of service. Workmen's trains between Chester and Broughton & Brotton, continued until September 1963. *Michael Mensing*

▼ With a somewhat grubby train, tired-looking surroundings and staff dressed in the uniform of the age, this animated scene somehow captures the British Railways era towards the end of the steam age. Note particularly the regulation headgear of the train guard and driver. This illustration features Northampton Castle station with Fowler 2-6-4T No 42381 about to depart with the 6.12pm to Wellingborough on 17 June 1961. Passenger services over the route and on to Peterborough (East) were withdrawn in May 1964. *Michael Mensing*

▲ For many decades the Welsh valley lines were infested by large numbers of 0-6-2T steam locomotives; however, slowly but surely, the march of progress continued as dieselisation took hold. This green-liveried three-car DMU is seen idling at Ebbw Vale on 23 April 1962 before running down the valley with the 1.35pm to Aberbeeg, where connections for Newport would be provided. The branch closed to passengers a few days later, although most of the line continued to be used by steel and coal trains. The steel works closed in 2002, but miraculously, the branch reopened to passengers in February 2008, albeit not to the now-demolished station seen here. *Michael Mensing*

▼ Further down the valley from Ebbw Vale is Aberbeeg, which was the junction for lines to Abertillery, Nantyglo and Brynmawr. Both on the Ebbw Vale branch and the Abertillery line there were once large numbers of collieries with a vast array of sidings provided at Aberbeeg for holding and marshalling coal wagons. Although the Ebbw Vale branch has been reopened there is presently no station at Aberbeeg. This was the scene on 23 April 1962 and for the next quarter of a century diesel mechanical units would operate most valley services. This is the 2.33pm from Ebbw Vale. *Michael Mensing*

▲ Although mixed trains on branch and minor lines had all but disappeared by the 1960s, in a handful of areas the odd van or milk tanker was attached to a service DMU. This shiny two-car unit has an old SR four-wheeled utility van as a tail load, probably containing post and/or parcels traffic. The 4.47pm Cambridge to Bletchley is seen at Sandy, Bedfordshire, on the Cambridge to Oxford cross-country line on 7 August 1961, this train being a 'short' working to Bletchley. Although closed to passengers in January 1968, except for the Bedford to Bletchley section, this is one of the lines that is mooted by optimists for reopening as part of a London orbital route. *Michael Mensing*

▼ These 'Derby Lightweight' units date back to July 1956, and were built for use on the Banbury (Merton Street) to Buckingham and Bletchley service. The exhaust pipes from the 150hp BUT(AEC) diesel engine ran to the roof line on an alignment between the cab windows at one end of the unit. Nos M79901 and M79900 are seen at Brackley on 6 August 1960 with the 3.45pm from Banbury to Buckingham, a service that was withdrawn from January 1961. The lead unit was withdrawn in December 1966, while the second unit eventually entered departmental service and survives in preservation. *Michael Mensing*

▶ The town of East Grinstead had the benefit of north to south and east to west rail routes. To accommodate these lines there were linked high- and low-level stations. Today, the only survivor is an electrified line from London and Croydon via Oxted, which terminates at what was the low-level station. The east to west route ran from Three Bridges to Tunbridge Wells West, but the line closed from January 1967. On a grey, misty and damp 17 December 1966 the 12.55 from Tunbridge Wells West is seen arriving at the high-level station. The DEMU is 'Oxted' unit No 1307. Three enthusiasts take snaps from the window of the train, something they would not be able to do two weeks later. *Author*

▶ This shows the same view as the previous photograph just 18 months later. While the platform edges remain, all track has been ripped up and the signalbox and other buildings demolished. Eventually the whole area would be ripped out for a new road scheme. In the foreseeable future, the well-established Bluebell Railway is hoping to be running trains into East Grinstead, with a link-up with the national rail network providing the potential for visits by through trains. *Author*

▶ This delightful little LBSCR signalbox was located at the east end of the single-platform Grange Road station on the Three Bridges to East Grinstead and Tunbridge Wells West line. A nice touch is the old tapered gas lamp and the access ladder, not to mention the neat row of red fire buckets. *Author*

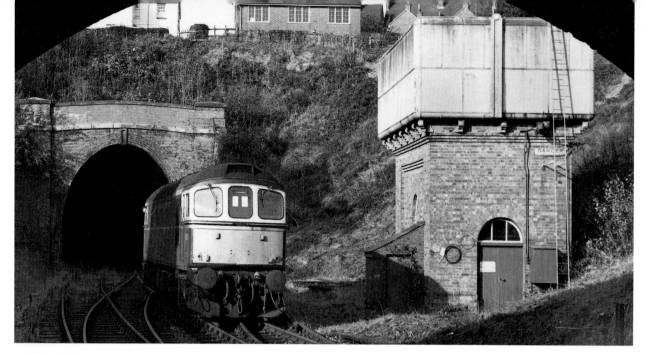

▲ Part of the so-called 'Cuckoo Line' dated back to May 1849, when the Polegate to Hailsham branch opened. The route from Hailsham was finally opened through to Eridge in 1880, and soon trains were running from Eastbourne to Tunbridge Wells West. The line opened in stages and over 80 years later it was to close in stages, the passenger service between Hailsham and Polegate finally being withdrawn on 8 September 1968. Although the line from Hailsham to Eridge closed in June 1965, coal traffic continued to run from Polegate to Heathfield until April 1968. Here Class 33/2 'Slim Jim' No D6597 (later No 33212) runs round its freight in the abandoned Heathfield station in 1967. *Author*

◄ On 10 November 1966, 3H 'Hampshire' DEMU No 1118 pauses at the isolated Brooklands Halt with an Ashford to New Romney train. The passing loop here was removed in 1921; note the old platform on the right. The signalbox was also demolished and this crossing signal was controlled from a small nearby hut. At this stage the line was doomed, closing to passengers in March 1967, although this part of the line is still open for occasional nuclear flask traffic. *Author*

◄ Early views of DMUs and DEMUs without any form of yellow warning panel now look remarkably dated. Another sign of times past is the pile of GPO mail bags and parcels on the platform, which had just been unloaded from the inbound working, not to mention the large barrow to transport them. On 10 November 1966 the 11.05am to Eastbourne in the form of 3H unit No 1114 prepares to leave Hailsham. The station has now been razed, the track lifted and the Cuckoo Trail along the old trackbed is available for walkers, cyclists and equestrian traffic. *Author*

▲ Once upon a time there was a through passenger service from Manchester to Macclesfield via Gorton and Romiley on the old Great Central & North Staffordshire Joint line. However, this was cut back to Rose Hill (Marple) from January 1970 and the line south of the town closed completely. The redundant track was removed and here we see a Class 104 DMU ready to leave a rationalised Rose Hill (Marple) for Manchester Piccadilly on 30 June 1973. *Gavin Morrison*

▼ A great photographic rarity is an all-green-liveried, Scottish Region allocated, English Electric Type 1 (Class 20) fitted with tablet catching equipment, trundling along a now-abandoned branch line with a typical pick-up goods. No D8034 (later No 20034) was photographed near Lumphanan on the Ballater branch on 13 July 1964 with a wonderfully mixed load. The last year that trains ran along these metals was 1966. *Michael Mensing*

◄ After passenger services were withdrawn between Rugby and Leamington Spa in 1959 freight continued to run between Rugby and Southam & Long Itchington (reversing at Marton Junction), where there was a Rugby Portland Cement works, but that all ended from August 1985. BR Sulzer Type 2 (Class 24) No D5137 (later No 24137) is seen on the by then freight-only line about half a mile west of Southam, on 21 June 1966, with a load of coal aboard the 12.33pm from Rugby. The locomotive is in green livery with a small yellow warning panel. *Michael Mensing*

◄ Featured here is a branch train working in the tiny county of Rutland. Until closure in June 1960 (goods 1964) there was a former LNWR 3½-mile branch line from Seaton to Uppingham. At Seaton there were services to Market Harborough and Stamford, the latter route joining the (still open) former Midland Railway line between Leicester and Peterborough near Luffenham. However, Seaton to Stamford services were axed in June 1966. Making a determined effort to maintain time the driver of the 5.57pm to Stamford keeps the regulator of Standard 2-6-2T No 84008 open as a two-coach formation passes underneath the MR line from Manton Junction to Corby and Kettering on 27 March 1965. *Michael Mensing*

◄ The Horncastle branch in Lincolnshire opened in 1855 and was one of the many lines where goods traffic long survived the withdrawal of passenger services. Low usage resulted in passenger trains being axed in September 1954, but freight in the shape of fuel tanks continued to trundle along the branch, latterly thrice weekly as required, until April 1971. Towards the end of its days the service was uneconomic as a diesel shunter and brakevan had to work their loads all the way from Lincoln, taking to the branch at Woodhall Junction. Here, Class 10 No D4075 (withdrawn in April 1972) passes a rural crossing in April 1970 with the train crew operating the gates. This part of the branch is now a footpath. *Author*

▲ The Suffolk terminus of Aldeburgh opened in 1860, but in this 1963 shot it looks to be heavily rationalised and there is a pile of recovered track stacked in the erstwhile goods yard, which had closed in 1959. A whiskered Metropolitan Cammell Class 101 unit pauses under the overall roof before running to Saxmundham, something it would no longer do after September 1966. Approximately weekly nuclear traffic still runs to sidings for Sizewell Power Station, near Leiston. *Author's collection*

▼ During your author's visits to an immense variety of branch lines the train crews were often cooperative in agreeing to pause a moment for an avid enthusiast travelling on their train to obtain a photograph. From the enthusiast's point of view such an occasion may well have been the last opportunity to record a branch before closure. Curious railway staff watch the photographer's antics in the pouring rain at Cressing, on the Witham to Braintree & Bocking branch. As already mentioned, the line did not wither but blossomed, eventually being electrified. *Author*

▲ Most railfans are well aware that there are open branch lines from Norwich to both Lowestoft (Central) and Yarmouth (Vauxhall), the latter via either Reedham or Acle. Another branch runs from Norwich to Cromer and Sheringham. However, now almost forgotten is the fact that until closed in May 1970, there was a direct passenger service between Yarmouth (South Town) and Lowestoft (Central). In this 1969 photograph a Class 101 DMU, with trailer car No E56054 leading, prepares to leave South Town. Note the old goods loading gauge that is still in situ, even though the track has been lifted, and also the ladies sitting in first-class accommodation! *Author*

▼ This more general view of Firsby shows all three platforms to advantage as well as the impressive station roof. This was an important interchange point with trains running to and from Lincoln, Boston and Sleaford, Skegness, Mablethorpe, Louth and Grimsby, not to mention a branch line to Spilsby that closed in September 1939. A Grimsby Town train is on the left while a terminating train from Lincoln via Woodhall Junction is on the right. Again, 'Gentlemen' seem to be well catered for and the station garden needs a little tlc! *Author*

▶ Although at one time a common sight on former Great Northern Railway lines, to the visitor there was something fascinating about GN somersault signals. One of their last bastions was in Lincolnshire, including the Skegness line. This 1969 study shows the up starting signal at Firsby, looking towards Bellwater Junction and Boston, while the spur onto the Skegness line is on the left. There is now no trace of the railway at this site, all lines having closed in 1970, except for the nearby Sleaford to Skegness via Boston line in the far distance. *Author*

▲ The area around Ironbridge has great significance in terms of the Industrial Revolution in the UK, especially iron foundries. Just to the north of Ironbridge is Coalbrookdale and having crossed Coalbrookdale Viaduct in the background, single power car No W55012 is seen passing the town with the 5.50pm Wellington to Much Wenlock on 9 June 1962. Sadly, the line closed to passengers later in the month, although coal trains still pass the spot on their way to and from the power station at Ironbridge. *Michael Mensing*

▼ The branch line from Maiden Newton to Bridport ran through some delightful rolling Dorset countryside until complete closure in May 1975. The line was one of the last to close as a direct result of the 1963 Reshaping Plan report. Opened in 1857 the original line was built to broad gauge but converted to standard gauge in 1874. An extension to West Bay opened in 1878, but closed to passengers in 1930 and to goods in 1962. Goods services on the remaining branch were withdrawn three years later. This single power car had just worked train 2B96 in from the junction. Since 1901 the population of Bridport has increased from 5,700 to 13,000, but most rely on four wheels. Note the track rationalisation in this 1969 view. *Author*

STEAM TO DIESEL TRANSITION

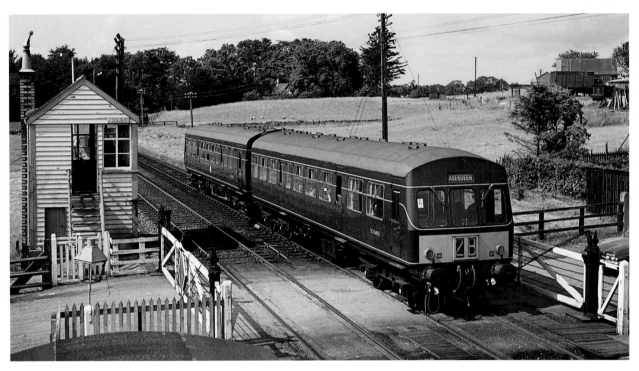

▲ The Ballater branch was famous for its associations with royalty, especially HM Queen Victoria and the splendid royal residence of Balmoral. The line opened in stages, from Aberdeen to Banchory in 1853, Banchory to Aboyne in 1859 and through to Ballater in 1866. A plan to extend the line to Braemar and even Inverness never materialised. On 17 July 1964 it was not a Royal Train but a humble DMU forming the 10.03am from Ballater to Aberdeen that arrived at Park station. *Michael Mensing*

▼ During the 1960s there was a gradual transition from steam to diesel traction on the surviving branches and minor lines. On 15 July 1965, the old Caledonian Railway tank engines on the Ballachulish branch had long been replaced by more modern power. In this view at the terminus a dirty Birmingham RCW Class 27 No D5363 (later No 27017) seems to be ready to depart with the 4.20pm to Oban, even though the photograph was taken at 2pm! There is a splendid backdrop to the general scene. *Michael Mensing*

▲ Featured again, but this time in colour, is the remote branch from Montrose to Inverbervie, which appears on some maps as just plain 'Bervie'. On 8 July 1964, J37 class 0-6-0 No 64608 is seen at the rarely photographed hamlet of Gourdon with a couple of box vans and a brakevan on the pick-up goods from Montrose. Unsurprisingly, the end was nigh and within two years the line was defunct. The footplate crew pose from the cab for the photographer. *Michael Mensing*

▼ Here we see the spacious terminus of Oban in Argyllshire on 20 May 1960. In Scottish Gaelic the word Oban means 'The Little Bay'. After running round its train ex-Caledonian Railway 0-4-4T No 55238 heads the empty stock of the 3.57pm from Ballachulish out of the station to the sidings. Top left is McCraig's Tower, a local landmark and folly with an impressive 650ft circumference that was built between 1897 and 1902. Due to McCraig's death it was never finished. *Michael Mensing*

► Although most branch goods trains had a booked path that usually appeared in the freight working timetables, the precise running times varied widely, sometimes resulting in a lengthy wait by the photographer. Occasionally, the working would be cancelled without the photographer's knowledge, but the worst scenario was when the safari was abandoned only for the train to appear shortly after the camera had been put away. Certainly if you missed this train there would not be another that day. On 30 May 1962 the lunchtime Tweedmouth to St Boswell's freight, comprising coal and cattle wagons, leaves Kelso behind Mogul 2-6-0 No 46479. *Michael Mensing*

▼ In the early 1960s, the Kircudbright branch was worked by LMS and BR Standard 2-6-4T locomotives as well as tender engines, including LMS 'Black Five' 4-6-0s. On 11 July 1963 it was a Fairburn-designed example in the shape of No 42689 that crossed over Tongland Bridge between Kircudbright and Tarff with the 4.51pm to Dumfries. Passenger and freight traffic ceased in 1965. *Michael Mensing*

▲ This image encapsulates what a country branch line is all about: a GWR steam locomotive, thinly populated maroon stock, single track, delightful scenery, and except for the engine's exhaust, complete tranquillity. Class 5101 large Prairie 2-6-2T No 4107 and leading coach No W2207W approach Lee Line Tunnel east of Mitcheldean Road station with the 4.30pm Hereford to Gloucester on 15 May 1964. *Michael Mensing*

▼ Wilmcote in Warwickshire is located between Bearley Junction and Stratford-upon-Avon. Trains heading to and from Birmingham via Solihull or the North Warwickshire line pass the station, as does traffic heading towards Warwick. Today, the route would fall into the minor line rather than branch line category, but before the line to Cheltenham closed it would have been described as a cross-country line. Looking truly magnificent in the late afternoon sunlight, 'Modified Hall' No 7918 *Rhose Wood Hall* heads a southbound mixed freight just north of the station, on 12 October 1963. *Michael Mensing*

▲ The Victorian railway builders did not do things by half, exemplified by this remarkable terminus at Alnwick in Northumberland. An alloy and glass bus shelter, which today's operators regard as sufficient for passengers, would not have been tolerated in those now far-off days. Steam traction was about to end on the branch from Alnmouth and, on 21 May 1966, K1 class 2-6-0 No 62050 looks to have been somewhat titivated for the occasion. By February 1968 there would be no trains of any description calling at Alnwick (see also page 64). *Gavin Morrison*

▼ This super picture records the scene at Stanhope station on the Weardale branch, which between Wearhead and Etherley (including Stanhope), closed to passengers in June 1953. Freight continued for a while, a civil engineer's tip at Etherley and the Eastgate Blue Circle Cement Works being the main sources of traffic. This RCTS special, headed by preserved K4 class 2-6-0 No 3442 (BR No 61994) *The Great Marquess* had made its way from Bishop Auckland and was heading for the truncated terminus at St John's on 11 June 1965. 'Presflo' cement wagons and a cement lorry are in the siding. *Gavin Morrison*

▲ The four-mile Wolverton to Newport Pagnell branch line in Buckinghamshire opened to goods traffic in 1866 and to passengers the following year. By 1901 the population of Newport Pagnell had reached 4,000, but within a few years motorised omnibuses began to offer competition in the area. The branch became a victim of the Beeching cuts and despite fierce local opposition the line closed to passengers in September 1964, and to goods in 1967. Here, Ivatt 2-6-2T No 41222 propels its train away from Great Linford station with the 1.30pm from the terminus to Wolverton on 26 October 1963. *Michael Mensing*

▼ A special version of the enthusiasts' railtour was a brakevan special where lines were explored from the veranda of one of these, usually 20-ton, vehicles. Although a handful remain in service there would be few, if any, locations where ten brakevans could be found, and in any event, in this day and age health and safety officials would no doubt regard the activity as potentially lethal! On 29 October 1966 the West Midlands branch of the RCTS organised a brakevan tour of the Stoke-on-Trent area and here we see the special headed by 2MT 2-6-2T No 41204 about a mile from Cauldon Quarry on the North Staffordshire Railway's matrix of lines north-east of the city. *Michael Mensing*

▲ A flash of sunshine illuminates this Gloucester RCW DMU as it departs from Seaton station with the 8.15am to Stamford on 28 May 1966. The photographer had made a special pilgrimage to the line, which closed just one week later. Sadly, but predictably, a large number of empty seats can be seen through the window, although this would not be the case on the last day of passenger service. *Michael Mensing*

▼ London Midland Region totem signs welcome passengers to Barnt Green station, junction for the Redditch branch. After the passenger service beyond Redditch to Evesham and Ashchurch officially closed in June 1963 the former station became the terminus of the line, a situation that prevails today. In a wonderful splash of colour this Park Royal Class 103 DMU with No M50395 leading, pauses at the station in 1964 on its way from Birmingham New Street to Redditch. A new station was subsequently built at Redditch and the line was electrified. *Michael Mensing*

▲ This panorama shows the slightly unusual junction station of St Ives, Cambridgeshire in July 1969. The line and platform to the left originally continued to Huntingdon and Kettering (closed 1959) whereas the two tracks on the right served the routes to Ely (closed 1931), and March (closed 1967), respectively. By this time the station was a terminus for trains from Cambridge and this Cravens DMU is seen returning to the university city. On the right are the sand hoppers for Fen Drayton (see page 66). *Author*

▼ The passenger service from Norwich to Wells-next-the-Sea was cut back to Dereham in October 1964 and closed between Dereham and Wymondham in October 1969. Freight continued to run to Fakenham and Ryburgh for some time. Three months before closure this Norwich-bound Class 101 DMU pauses for custom, and a photograph at Hardingham station. An alighting passenger can just be detected. Much of the line has now been restored and seasonal services are run by the Mid-Norfolk Railway. *Author*

▲ Throughout the 1960s the steam-to-diesel transition was rapidly taking place with some areas being dieselised almost *en bloc*. East Anglia was an early victim as BR cleared out large numbers of ancient steam locomotives and rolling stock. On 9 July 1969, Cromer station still boasted goods yard sidings and a seemingly large stock of coal. At many locations local coal merchants continued to use the railway goods yards, even though the coal was brought in by road! With the rear carriages of this four-car DMU under the overall roof, this formation will shortly be departing for Norwich. A supermarket was later built on the goods yard site. *Author*

▼ One of the most isolated branch line stations in East Anglia is Berney Arms. The tiny halt is the only intermediate stopping place between Yarmouth and Reedham. The flat marshland landscape once supported dozens of windmills but nearly all have now been replaced by new land-management technology. Only a couple of trains per day in each direction stop at the halt, by request only. The nearest road is over two miles distant and the Berney Arms pub on the River Yare is about two-thirds of a mile from the station, although easily accessible by boat. In this view the impossible seems to have happened as a mother and child alight from a Norwich-bound DMU. The scene is little changed today, except for new signs. *Author*

▲ To the layman, Wrexham seemed to be overrun with stations, with the railway map showing Central, Exchange and General, in addition to various halts. However, they all served a multitude of lines that operated in the area. One of the routes was the Cambrian Railway line from Wrexham to Ellesmere, which was cut back to Wrexham Central in September 1962. Before such rationalisation, 1400 class 0-4-2T No 1438 is seen calling at Hightown Halt, between Marchwiel and Wrexham Central, while propelling the 4.20pm from Ellesmere. The line from Central to Exchange (adjacent to General station) remains open. *Michael Mensing*

◄ The old Midland Railway branch line from Coaley on the Bristol to Birmingham main line, to the little market town of Dursley in Gloucestershire, closed to passengers in September 1962, but goods traffic continued for a further eight years, until July 1970. There was an intermediate station at Cam. Just nine weeks before years of history came to an end, Ivatt 2-6-0 No 46527 worked the 2.25pm Coaley to Dursley and is seen about half a mile from its destination. *Michael Mensing*

▲ Having already illustrated the Ebbw Vale branch and the Aberbeeg area in early diesel days, it seemed appropriate to reproduce a colour transparency from the last days of steam. Starting its climb out of Aberbeeg, albeit with only two coaches, pannier tank No 8786 makes for Ebbw Vale with the 5pm departure on 23 April 1962. The train would soon be passing Marine Colliery, coal and steel being the main freight commodities over the line. *Michael Mensing*

▼ One of the most interesting cross-country lines was the old Stratford-upon-Avon & Midland Junction Railway that ran from Blisworth and Towcester via Fenny Compton to Stratford-upon-Avon and Broom. The 45¾-mile journey was slow with lengthy stops (particularly at Stratford-upon-Avon) with no express through train running. Passenger services were withdrawn between 1949 and 1952 but freight traffic continued. This LCGB special traversed the route on 12 October 1963 and the 'Thames, Avon & Severn Rail Tour' is seen here west of Byfield behind a pair of six-coupled locomotives, 4300 class No 6368 and 2251 class No 2246. Only a short section of track from Fenny Compton to the MoD depot at Kineton remains. *Michael Mensing*

▲ Returning to the green DMU era, in this view a three-car Swindon cross-country Class 120 DMU is seen running past Oldland Common with the 5.55pm from Bath (Green Park) to Bristol (Temple Meads) on 13 May 1964. At Bath (Green Park) the train would have connected with the Somerset & Dorset route from Templecombe and Bournemouth West. The S&D finally closed in March 1966 and this old Midland Railway route closed in sympathy at the same time. *Michael Mensing*

▼ The GWR route to Barnstaple (Victoria) was from Taunton via Dulverton. Near Dulverton a junction was made with the Exe Valley branch to Stoke Canon and Exeter St David's. The line skirted the southern fringe of Exmoor and there were few centres of significant population. The Exe Valley line closed in October 1963 and the Barnstaple to Taunton line closed completely in October 1966. An immaculate two-car Class 118 suburban DMU is seen emerging from the tunnel and arriving at Venn Cross station with the 1.28pm from Taunton, on 23 June 1965 (see also page 74). *Michael Mensing*

▲ The atmosphere of the country branch line is encapsulated in this appealing study of the Culm Valley Light Railway at Uffculme in June 1972. Steam locomotives, pilot scheme diesels and passenger trains have long since disappeared from the line, and it is BR Sulzer Type 2 (Class 25) No D7502 (later No 25152) that approaches the level-crossing gates with the daily milk empties. On the left is Small's grain mill, a source of railway traffic for many years. As already mentioned, passenger trains ceased in September 1963 and freight, in the shape of milk traffic, petered out on 31 October 1975. *Author*

▲ The town of Brecon was approached from two directions by two different railway companies, the Neath & Brecon and the Brecon & Merthyr railways. Both ran through rugged country around the Brecon Beacons. December 1962 was a bleak time for the ancient town of Brecon, because passenger services ceased on all of the lines in the vicinity, leaving the town rail-less. The photographer was fortunate to capture two locomotives in a single frame at Brecon station on 10 September 1962. In the turntable siding is 0-6-0PT No 9631, while in the bay platform Collett 0-6-0 No 3201 is ready to leave for Moat Lane Junction. *Gavin Morrison*

◄ By 1965 the old Chichester to Midhurst line comprised merely a freight-only stub as far as Lavant, where the last general goods traffic was seasonal sugar beet. This traffic ceased in later years but a new aggregates terminal was opened nearby. On 3 October 1965 the line was included in the itinerary of the LCGB 'Vectis Farewell Tour', with participants going on to visit the Isle of Wight. Q1 class No 33027 nears Lavant with another Q1 at the rear of the train to obviate the need to run round. *Gavin Morrison*

▲ Thousands upon thousands of holidaymakers, particularly the older generation, will have happy memories of summer vacations at the seaside, which often involved a ride along a branch line. Swanage, Lyme Regis, Seaton, Sidmouth, Exmouth and Kingsbridge were just a few examples on the south coast. This scene from the summer of 1962 features the Swanage branch with the footplate crew of M7 0-4-4T No 30111 engaged in conversation before returning to Wareham. Having been opened in 1885 the line closed from 3 January 1972 (except for freight traffic to Furzebrook), but there was to be a happy ending when it became the Swanage Railway preserved line. This not only resulted in a successful tourist operation but more recently, reconnection to the main line. *Gavin Morrison*

▼ Ventnor terminus was a very special place in that immediately the single line exited the tunnel under St Boniface Down it fanned out into a versatile site with an attractive station, multiple sidings, and goods yard, plus all of the usual infrastructure items ranging from a signalbox to this water column. O2 class No 35 *Freshwater* takes water before returning bunker first to Ryde Pier Head. The line from Shanklin to Ventnor closed in April 1966. The telephone box looks to be in a rather perilous position and one wonders whether the lady occupant can hear her caller over the noise of the Westinghouse brake. *Gavin Morrison*

▲ It is often forgotten that in many locations, even in the 1960s, there were a large number of electrified branch lines. This particularly applied around London, throughout the suburban Southern Region, in the North East around Tyneside, and in parts of the North West ranging from Merseyside to Hadfield. Included in the list were the 'Morecambe Electrics', which had a history dating back to 1908. The original units were withdrawn in 1951 but by 1953/54 some old stored LNWR/LMS Metropolitan Carriage Wagon & Finance Co EMUs were resuscitated and modified for use between Heysham, Morecambe and Lancaster via Green Ayre. One of four three-car units, No M29021M, is ready to leave Morecambe Promenade for Lancaster on 9 October 1965. The electrified lines closed and the units were withdrawn from 3 January 1966. *Gavin Morrison*

▼ The old Midland Railway branch line from Skipton to Grassington & Threshfield, two attractive Wharfedale villages, was a casualty of the great depression, closing to passengers from 22 September 1930. However, goods traffic continued to use the whole line until August 1969. Subsequently, freight trains ran only from Skipton to Swinden lime works/Tilcon at Rylestone. On 16 June 1968, the RCTS arranged a special over the branch and Class 24 No D5113 (later No 24113) is seen arriving at Grassington with train 1Z44. The stationmaster seems to be officiating. *Gavin Morrison*

BR BLUE SUCCESSION

▲ This volume is about branch and minor lines and not a detailed survey of train liveries; suffice to say that from the mid-1960s onwards, standard BR blue, and blue and grey livery were gradually introduced. Also, the BR double-arrow sign became the standard logo, appearing on everything from locomotives to units, on rolling stock, signs and even rail tickets. An early version of blue livery with white roof and small yellow warning panel adorns this DMU seen at Bishops Lydeard station while working from Minehead to Taunton on 4 March 1969. The line closed from January 1971, but thankfully it is now the home of the West Somerset Railway. *Author*

▶ Also in March 1969 this blue single power car with full yellow cab ends was photographed at the little Combe Junction station on the Liskeard to Looe branch line in Cornwall. All branch trains reverse direction at this location, although not all trains run as far as the platform to perform the task. The route is rich in history and the track parallels the old Liskeard & Looe Union Canal down to the harbour at Looe (see page 10). Loadings are seasonal and in the summer months the train service is well used by visitors to Looe, who are encouraged to 'park and ride' at Liskeard. Note the lovely old sign and the chocolate and cream paint on the waiting hut. *Author*

▲ This page is dedicated to the lovers of lupins, whether they be in the Thames Valley or deepest Devon. The Thames Valley is still rich in branch lines with Windsor, Marlow and Henley all being served by train. In this June 1971 photograph a two-car DMU is seen approaching Wargrave station while working from Henley-on-Thames to Twyford. Over the years there have been regular timetabled through trains to London, Paddington, especially at 'commuter times'. Opened in June 1857 the branch was originally built to broad-gauge dimensions. *Author*

▼ Although in recent decades the line from Exeter St David's to Barnstaple, now known as the 'Tarka Line', has primarily been in the hands of diesel units, there have been locomotive-hauled trains on the branch, including summer Saturday through trains from London, Paddington. Other non-unit trains have included those with a dual parcels and passenger role, and in the mid-1980s there was even a through working to Penzance. In this June 1971 view at Copplestone an Exeter-bound three-car DMU looks resplendent in grey and blue livery. The line is still open and business is brisk. On balance it appears that the Wargrave lupins are superior! *Author*

▶ Windsor & Eton is a popular destination for visitors. Whether it be the old town centre, the castle and St George's Chapel, the River Thames, the theatre, or the playing fields of Eton, there is plenty to see in the area. The town is served by what was once the Western Region of BR from Slough to Central station and by the Southern Region from Staines and Richmond to Riverside station. In this June 1971 study at Central a two-car hybrid formation will soon leave for the short run to Slough. *Author*

◀ Although a four-car DMU formation was provided on the Bridport branch line for the last day of service in May 1975, this view recorded a month before closure features the standard motive power on the line during its last decade of existence. The number of seats provided by the single car was more than adequate. On a pleasant spring day a lunchtime train heading for the junction at Maiden Newton approaches Toller Porcorum. *Author*

▶ This rather bleak scene from July 1971 is at Severn Beach at the end of the branch line from Bristol Temple Meads via Stapleton Road, Montpelier and Avonmouth (see page 2). The station building on the left was unusual in being set at right angles to the railway, fronting the access road behind the gates. The line to the right once continued to Pilning, east of the Severn Tunnel. The running-in board seems to have collapsed but the GWR seats remain as a reminder of the past. *Author*

▲ The former Great Eastern Railway terminus of Southminster is featured here, in February 1973. A three-car DMU stands at the platform before returning to the junction station of Wickford, 16½ miles away. At this time, semaphore signalling survived; indeed, the photograph was taken from the signalbox. The light-coloured material covering the foreground tracks is sand that has leaked from hopper wagons that were loaded nearby. The line prospered and was included in an electrification scheme, ensuring its long-term survival. *Author*

▼ This Ipswich-bound Cravens unit is pausing at Trimley station on the 1877 Felixstowe branch. The branch from Westerfield, the junction for the East Suffolk line, became part of the Great Eastern Railway in 1887. Many years ago the line ran directly to Felixstowe Town station, where a reversal was necessary to reach Felixstowe Beach and Pier. This 'extension' closed in 1951 (Pier to Beach) and 1967 (Beach to Town). All of this was overshadowed by the rapid development of Felixstowe container port, the largest in the UK, which has included a new railway spur from the old branch line to the dock area, resulting in significant freight volumes along part of the line. *Author*

▲ When photographed in July 1971 the rather grand Great Eastern Railway terminus building at North Woolwich housed a museum given over to railway relics from the GER. At this time most trains, including this DMU, ran to Stratford and in peak hours to Tottenham Hale. In 1985, the line was electrified by third rail, effectively forming part of the old North London Line route through to Richmond in Surrey. The line closed in 2005, being incorporated in other transport developments in the area between Stratford and the Docklands area of east London (see page 80). *Author*

▼ There has been rationalisation at Braintree & Bocking station in this July 1971 view. Abandoned platforms can be seen on the left, reflecting the fact that until March 1952 the line beyond once continued to Bishop's Stortford via Rayne, Felstead, Dunmow, Easton Lodge and Takeley. The driver of the DMU has time for a chat with the signalman as a lady passenger and her shopping trolley join the train for the ride to Witham. As already mentioned, the line was subsequently electrified, providing a through train service to London, Liverpool Street. *Author*

E56083

▲ The name of the Northumberland town of Haltwhistle has nothing to do with the coming of the railway. The name is derived from *Hal-Twysel,* 'a meeting of streams by the hill'. In fact, the town of about 4,000 inhabitants is located in the valley of the South Tyne River. Until May 1976, the station was the junction for the Alston branch, although this side of the running-in board faced passengers arriving from Alston. The bold orange and white sign reflects the colours used by the North Eastern Region of British Railways. *Author*

▼ This damp scene is at the intermediate station of Lambley on the then doomed Alston branch. The train, comprising a two-car Metro-Cammell Class 101 DMU, has just crossed the impressive Lambley Viaduct on its way to Alston. The track has a check rail added through the curved station platform. The trackbed here is now part of the 23-mile South Tyne Trail. At Alston, the narrow-gauge South Tynedale Railway has been operating since 1983. *Author*

◀ Stranraer is located at the end of Loch Ryan in Wigtownshire, at the south-western tip of Scotland, 101 miles by rail from Glasgow Central. The present terminus is at Stranraer Harbour, the line to Stranraer Town and Portpatrick having closed in March 1966. There are regular sailings from the harbour to Larne in Northern Ireland. In this 1974 study, a Swindon Class 120 three-car DMU is Glasgow bound while fuel tankers on the left and parcel vans on the right enrich the train variety. The line remains open. *Author*

◀ April 2000 brought an end to a remarkable phenomenon at Nairn station, on the line from Aberdeen to Inverness. The station was the last to retain the Highland Railway practice of having a signalbox at each end of a passing loop, but with the instruments and control levers in the station buildings. This necessitated the signalman to furiously pedal a bicycle between the east and west boxes and the main building every time a train arrived. However, in 2000, Westrace interlocking was installed that was controlled only from the station building, ending the idiosyncrasy seen here in 1974. *Author*

◀ The 4½-mile North Berwick branch leaves the Newcastle to Edinburgh main line at Drem. The line was opened throughout in 1850, and in the past there were two intermediate stations. Steam gave way to diesel in 1958 and in 1991 the branch was generating sufficient traffic to justify the cost of electrification. However, back in September 1975 it was a humble Class 101 DMU that waited at the terminus for the right away to Edinburgh Waverley. A fine floral display greets passengers. *Author*

▲ During 1988, the 6½-mile former LNWR branch from Watford Junction to St Albans Abbey was another to be electrified. Prior to electrification, a Cravens unit leaves the much rationalised station for Watford during April 1973. A miserable brick shelter provides the only passenger comfort. Opened in 1858, the branch pre-dated the Midland Railway main line and their St Albans City station on the other side of town by a full ten years. Prior to its closure in October 1951, the station was also served by a Great Northern Railway branch line from Hatfield. *Author*

▼ Few enthusiasts would ever have thought that Birmingham Snow Hill station, pride of the Great Western Railway in Britain's second city, would ever have appeared in a branch line book. However, by the time this photograph of a single power car DMU was taken in August 1971 nearly all key services had either been diverted to Birmingham New Street or discontinued altogether, leaving just local services to Wolverhampton Low level and Langley Green. These ended in March 1972 and Snow Hill closed. Stripped of its former grandeur it reopened in 1987 when the old GWR route became part of a cross-city transport system and the site is now thriving. *Author*

▶ The somewhat eccentric activities of railway enthusiasts, your author included, apparently knows no bounds! In June 1975 the St Albans branch of the LCGB organised an open coal wagon special along the line from Hemelite cement works at Claydale siding towards Harpenden. Participants had to climb ladders to board the shunter-hauled train. The line from Harpenden to Hemel Hempstead opened in 1877 but was closed to passengers by the LMS in 1947. The cement traffic continued until July 1979 and much of the trackbed is now a footpath. *Author*

▼ Built in 1879, this substantial and handsome but latterly unstaffed terminus building at Stourbridge Town, was demolished a century later, in 1979. The branch was also shortened by 70 yards and a new station constructed. For many years a single power car diesel unit shuttled backwards and forwards between Town and Junction stations where passengers changed for nationwide destinations, but mainly Birmingham, as seen here in August 1971. In the last year of BR operation there were over 70 shuttles along the ¾-mile branch in each direction every weekday. Goods services were withdrawn at Town during 1965 and the old alignment can be seen to the right of this DMU. In recent times the branch has been in the news as Parry People Mover vehicles have replaced conventional trains on the line. *Author*

▲ The two stations featured on this page both survive in name, but not in the precise locations illustrated. On a wretched day in June 1973, a two-car DMU is seen at Blackpool South before working to Kirkham & Wesham, where a connection will be made for Preston. In years gone by Blackpool catered for huge volumes of holiday traffic and, as can be seen beyond the bridge, acres upon acres of space between Blackpool South and Central were put to railway use, mainly as excursion train sidings. Blackpool North is now regarded as the main station. South station is now a featureless structure with a short modern platform (see page 212). *Author*

▼ The grand Midland Railway Morecambe Promenade station still exists but not for railway use. Instead, another featureless excuse for a station has been built some distance short of this site amidst supermarkets and fast-food outlets (see page 212). However, when viewed back in the 1970s it was still possible, perhaps through half-closed eyes, to envisage the scenes from the heydays of the British seaside resort. A Class 101 has just come to a halt while a shunter waits hopefully for its next turn of duty. The branch line from Morecambe to Heysham is still open, but the train service is sparse. *Author*

▲ Earlier in this volume the line between Wrexham Central and Ellesmere was featured during the days of steam (see page 114), but when photographed in October 1974 Wrexham Central, seen here, was the end of the line from Wrexham Exchange, just over half a mile distant. The line survives and the service is now approximately hourly with trains running through to Bidston. Yet again, rationalisation has been extreme, all on the grounds of reducing maintenance and running costs. *Author*

▼ It is very difficult these days to incorporate as many as 16 brick-built stacks in a single railway photograph but at Stewartby in Bedfordshire, brickworks and brick kilns appear in abundance. This site is now better known for inbound waste trains than outbound brick trains (see page 210). In May 1973, a Bedford to Bletchley Cravens-built DMU approaches the station and is seen passing an upper quadrant semaphore home signal. In terms of signalling and road crossing equipment this line has since been modernised. *Author*

◀ Whether in the steam or diesel era, most illustrations featured so far have depicted branch and minor lines in operation. However, photographs of the remains of railway infrastructure after closure of a line can generate sadness, invoke nostalgia and provide a fascinating insight into the fate of various sites. Such views normally needed to be captured within a few years of closure, otherwise vandalism and redevelopment could completely destroy a site. These were the remains of Heathfield station on the 'Cuckoo Line' in East Sussex (see pages 60 and 98) in September 1971, six years after closure to passengers, and three years after goods services were withdrawn. Nothing now survives, other than the old tunnel entrance. *Author*

◀ Looking north in June 1971 we see the gaunt shell of Fullerton Junction signalbox in Hampshire, with the decaying station in the background. The station was on the 'Spratt & Winkle Line' (a name also used elsewhere) from Romsey to Andover Junction and it was also the junction for the line to Longparish and Hurstbourne, on the right, which closed to passengers in July 1931. The echoes of a LSWR T9 class 4-4-0 or a 3H 'Hampshire' DEMU were by then very distant, the line having closed in September 1964. *Author*

◀ Baynards station in Surrey is featured here in March 1972, seven years after passenger services between Horsham and Guildford ceased. The railway was opened in 1865 and in this area it ran through Lord Thurlow's land. As a condition of sale of the land he insisted on his own station being built, and on a substantial scale. Nearby was a brick and tile works that was rail served. The station staff once tended a wonderful display of dahlias on the platform. The restored station building survives in private ownership. *Author*

▲ These two photographs show typical remains of the Pulborough to Midhurst branch line in West Sussex, which closed to passengers in 1955, but survived for goods until 1966. It looks as though the station awning at Fittleworth is about to collapse in this May 1972 view. However, it is pleasing to report that the station was eventually sold by the BR Property Board and restored by the new owner. This view is looking east, towards Hardham Junction. *Author*

▼ The author travelled on the last goods train from Petworth in May 1966. An extra brakevan was provided for three enthusiasts and in addition to the train crew of driver, second man and guard the area manager turned up for the auspicious occasion. As the train departed from Petworth, detonators exploded but when photographed in July 1971 that all seemed far off. Food and accommodation are now offered at the site in redundant but restored Pullman cars, perpetuating the railway connection at Petworth station, albeit some distance from the town. *Author*

◀ While in purely scenic terms they may not compare with branch lines in Cornwall or Scotland, there are a multitude of interesting electrified branch lines on the former Southern Region London suburban network that receive little publicity and seem to be shunned by railway photographers. In this leisurely August 1975 scene, 4-SUB electric unit No 4722, pauses at Epsom Downs terminus at the end of the branch from Sutton. Notice the oil tail lamp on an electric train and the semaphore signal. Opened in 1865 the station once had nine platforms, mostly for racegoers. Everything visible here was swept away in 1989 and a new station and single platform were built 300 yards nearer Sutton, with the released land being sold for housing. *Author*

▼ Morden Halt, later called Morden Road, was an intermediate stopping point on the Wimbledon to West Croydon via Mitcham Junction line. The line opened back in 1857, but 140 years later, in 1997, the line closed and was converted for use by trams under the Croydon Tramway system. A tram stop now occupies this site. Whirring along the single track is 2-EPB unit No 5790 with a train from Wimbledon, in February 1973. *Author*

▶ Although the public were made aware of impending branch line closures, there was always a startling realisation of the full implications of an announcement when actual closure notices were posted on stations. This shows the typical format of the dreaded document. Although there was a formal process to go through between the official announcement and the actual closure date these posters effectively activated a ticking clock counting down towards final abandonment. This example was posted on Corfe Castle station and was photographed in December 1971. *Author*

▼ With only three weeks of service left the signalman and the driver pose for the photographer with the single-line tokens, which after exchange and subsequent signalbox activity, will allow the train to proceed to Swanage. 'Hampshire' unit No 1125 was recorded with a down working from Wareham on 9 December 1971. Barely visible through the trees are the remains of Corfe Castle. It is heartening to know that the station now sees Swanage Railway trains at its platforms, 30 years after closure by BR, and 126 years after the branch first opened. *Author*

WITHDRAWAL OF RAILWAY PASSENGER SERVICE BETWEEN WAREHAM AND SWANAGE

The Southern Region of British Railways hereby give notice that on and from Monday 3 January 1972 the railway passenger service between Wareham and Swanage will be withdrawn and Corfe Castle and Swanage stations closed.

Details of the alternative bus services are available at local railway stations and bus offices.

British Rail | Southern

◀ With the rationalisation of the railways and the part closure of certain routes a number of erstwhile main lines effectively became branch lines. A good example of this was the former Southern route from Exeter to Plymouth. Passenger services between Bere Alston and Okehampton ceased in May 1968, resulting in Okehampton becoming a passenger terminus. Traffic to Meldon Quarry, beyond the town, continued. In June 1971, a year before passenger services were finally withdrawn, a single-car DMU is watched by a couple of track workers as it pauses at North Tawton on its way from Okehampton to Exeter St David's. Note the straight but undulating former main line alignment. *Author*

◀ Okehampton's status as a passenger train terminus did not last long as the closure notices for the remaining section from Yeoford were duly posted. The closure day approached and locals and enthusiasts made notes in their diaries that Saturday 3 June 1972 would be the last day of service. With a crowd of well-wishers and the Mayor and Mayoress in attendance, the last train from Okehampton to Exeter is about to leave the station. In later years, subsidised trains have run from Exeter to Okehampton on summer weekends and the Dartmoor Railway commenced a privatised train service on part of the route, so the scene here was not quite 'The End'. *Author*

◀ Another once-defunct branch line that now finds revenue-earning trains traversing its route is the Bodmin & Wenford Railway. With part of the route dating back to 1834 and with both Southern and Western Region origins, the old Wenford Goods train was routed via Boscarne Junction and Bodmin General rather than Boscarne and Wadebridge once the Southern routes closed. From 1983, all traffic ceased allowing, in due course, the preservationists to take over. In March 1974, No 08839, a brakevan and a single wagon of china clay, leave Bodmin General for Bodmin Road and St Blazey. On occasions, loads were left at Bodmin Road or, more usually, Boscarne Junction for 'tripping' to the main line by a larger engine. *Author*

1970s AND CONSOLIDATION

WITH THE HUGE NUMBER OF CLOSURES being undertaken in accordance with the 1963 Reshaping Plan some aspects of the process were under pressure, but as the railways could not, by law, simply 'pull the plug' on loss-making services, every stage of the proceedings had to be completed. Consequently, many lines remained open, although under threat of closure. Most of these closure proposals were effectively 'cut and dried'; as the lines were so little used there was no substantial defence that could be made against closure. However, as previously mentioned, the main criticisms at the public meetings were that the costings in the report could not be challenged, insufficient weight had been given to contributory income from the branches and minor lines, and no consideration had been given to social needs and resulting hardship if closure took place.

In the 1962 Act a Central Transport Consultative Committee was established to become a consumer body to represent users of the railway. In addition, a sub-structure of Area Transport Users Consultative Committees was established to cover individual areas of the country. The role of these committees was to make recommendations relating to the service provided on threatened lines and the public were encouraged to contact the TUCCs if they had objections to closure of any particular line. However, ultimately, the Minister of Transport was not bound to follow any of the TUCC recommendations. The procedure for closure was that British Railways was obliged to give six weeks' notice of their intention to close a line and to publish this proposal on two consecutive weeks in two local newspapers in the area affected.

Normally, closure notices were also posted on all relevant stations, giving the proposed date of closure. A copy of the notice was sent to the area TUCC committee. The adverts were obliged to provide details of alternative transport services (including any services that BR themselves were intending to provide) and invite members of the public to send objections to a specific address within the six-week period. Rail users affected by any closure could also send their objections to the TUCC who would then report to the Minister of Transport, recording the result of their deliberations and highlighting any 'hardship' that would occur as a result of the closure and recommend measures to ease that hardship. The closure would not be proceeded with until the Minister had given his consent. Based on the TUCC report the Minister would sometimes consent to a closure subject to certain conditions, such as assurances over alternative transport services.

Pre-closure meetings were frustrating for members of the public who could obviously not influence BR accounting practice. For example, it was obvious to many that the cost of maintaining a high-speed main line was significantly more expensive in cost per mile terms than keeping a rural single-track branch line in safe condition. BR did break down their track maintenance categories into four groups, rated from A to D. Each category had a fixed national unit cost that was applied to all lines in a given category, whether or not actual work had been carried out on a particular branch line. While one could understand the need for applying corporate unit costs it meant that a dead straight, well-drained branch line could be charged for maintenance at the same rate per mile as a line that was steeply graded, circuitous and subject to landslips!

Every railway enthusiast knew that the track on some branch lines had been in situ for many decades, demonstrating that there had been little inward investment and sometimes cast-iron chairs would show the name of pre-Grouping railway companies. As an example of line depreciation costs, the Alston branch from Haltwhistle carried an annual overhead of £77,000 before a single wheel on a train moved along the track. One can only imagine what the takings at the intermediate station of Slaggyford might have been, but they would certainly not cover a tiny fraction of such unrealistic fixed unit costs.

Also, the reshaping report failed to look ahead at probable future developments. For example, on the non-electrified line from Shoreham-by-Sea to Christ's Hospital (effectively a Brighton to Horsham service) in Sussex, the finances on a profit and loss basis were marginally on the debit side of the cost equation. The line closed in March 1966. However, population growth would see large housing estates built at Steyning, Henfield and Southwater, which almost certainly would have favourably tipped the scales on financial viability. Furthermore, while the commonly asked questions were dealt with in the report (see previous chapter), if in this case more economies had been made, for example singling the double-track line and the withdrawing of staff from intermediate stations, the route could well have become profit-making. It would of course be ridiculous to challenge some of the closure proposals where a single coach with a couple of passengers plied to and fro between remote rural stations, but in many cases the mathematics were marginal. In some areas bus replacement services simply did not exist, although on some of the longer routes buses quickly established themselves as a viable alternative, at least for 'through' passengers, such as that between Bude and Exeter via Okehampton. In 1965, a rail journey from Bude to Exeter St David's took (with changes) 2 hours 12 minutes, whereas in 2011 the bus takes 1 hour 45 minutes.

Every branch line closure had a story to tell and on occasions public pressure delayed the inevitable. Although it would be difficult to prove in a court of law it was the allegedly sneaky way in which some closures were manipulated that irritated the public. A common tactic was to timetable branch trains that almost seemed to avoid peak periods, and at junction stations important connections with main line trains were missed, sometimes by only a matter of minutes, a practice that continued long after Beeching. For example, prior to significant timetable changes in 2008, the first train out of Newquay in Cornwall was not until after 9am, thereby preventing anybody travelling to work by train. On the same line in 2000 a lunchtime train departed from the junction station of Par at 11.52 shortly before the first train of the day from London, Paddington, arrived at 12.14, leaving passengers with a two-hour wait!

Although taking place in the 1960s, the famous Somerset & Dorset line from Bournemouth West to Bath gave the impression of being closed by stealth. Services were gradually reduced and modern traction was not employed on the line, even at the time of closure in March 1966. Goods traffic (admittedly of the uneconomic variety) was gradually withdrawn and, worst of all, the many high season holiday trains that used the route on their way from the Midlands and the north of England to south coast resorts, such as the 'Pines Express' were diverted via other routes. Although the S&D was difficult to work, this latter move was cynical in the extreme. Needless to say, based on what was a substantially local service, the 77-mile line failed to survive and would never have passed a financial viability test in profit and loss terms.

One of the most significant changes in Government thinking occurred towards the end of the 1960s, but it was more relevant to the 1970s. This was the provision made in the 1968 Transport Act for the Minister of Transport to pay grants to the British Railways Board in respect of unremunerative railway lines where 'it is desirable for social or economic reasons that railway passenger services to and from the place or places in question should for the time being continue to be provided either in the same or in some different form or manner and that because of the unremunerative nature of the services which the Minister is satisfied as desirable for those reasons (hereafter in this section referred to as "required services") the Board cannot reasonably be expected to provide them without assistance under this section. The Minister may from time to time with the consent of the Treasury undertake to make grants to the Board in respect of the provision of the required services for such a period not exceeding three years or a time the Minister may think fit.'

The Act continued by affording the Minister the right to impose certain conditions on the provision of such services. The Minister, in consultation with the British Railways Board, had to fully account for the income received and expenditures made so as to provide the Treasury with an accurate figure of the grant (or to put it more crudely 'subsidy') required to continue running the service. The legal terminology is remarkable and worth recording, even though it may not win a 'plain English' award: '(so that the Minister) may determine that the expenditure properly attributable to the provision during that period of the required service will exceed the revenue properly so attributable; and payments in pursuance of the undertaking shall be made in such a manner and at such times as the Minister may with the approval of the Treasury determine'. The start date for the scheme was 1 January 1969.

In other words, for the first time it was recognised that there could be social, practical, or dare one say it, political reasons to keep a loss-making line open. Obviously there had to be close scrutiny of such cases because any subsidy would come out of the public purse, but as a matter of principle this section of the 1968 Act, which was mostly about other forms of transport, particularly buses and road transport, was groundbreaking. Also if a separate subsidy (or 'grant') was to be paid then the British Railways Board did not need to suffer any losses attributable to this source in their corporate accounts. If the Minister agreed that a grant was appropriate then any worries about the viability of a branch or minor line could be dispelled. Although by the 1970s the rate of line closures was bound to slow there was now a possible lifeline for some lines where the closure process had been protracted and the routes were still in existence and operating. There was a suggestion in the press that a line stood a better chance of survival if it so happened to be in a marginal constituency!

Despite this possible lifeline, line closures continued throughout the 1970s. Some examples included Kidderminster to Bewdley, Hartlebury to Bewdley, Bourne End to High Wycombe, Poulton-le-Fylde to Fleetwood, Barnstaple Junction to Ilfracombe, Marple Rose Hill to Macclesfield, Colne to Skipton, Lowestoft Central to Yarmouth South Town, Bridgend to Treherbert, Willoughby to Mablethorpe, Lincoln to Firsby via Tumby Woodside, Taunton to Minehead, Wareham to Swanage, Barry Island to Barry Pier, Wolverhampton Low Level to Birmingham Snow Hill, Bolton to Rawtenstall, Paignton to Kingswear, Maiden Newton to Bridport, Haltwhistle to Alston, the line to Filey Holiday camp, and West Monkseaton to Tynemouth.

One of the most important reviews of the state of the railways was the Government's 'Rail Policy Review' of 1974. This review took on board the state of British Railways, including the fall-out from both Beeching reports and the various Transport Acts and at report stage came up with arguably the most salient statement ever published on railway finances: 'The passenger business as a whole, at anything like its present size, is incapable of breaking even. The cost of the passenger system could not be reduced without service closures on a scale disproportionate to the expected savings.' There was a rider that gave the railways discretion and that was a recommendation that any grant paid should be for the passenger system (as a whole) and not on a service-by-service basis. This would still give the British Railways Board the opportunity to close lines, subject to the various processes.

By this time European legislation had to be taken on board, the law being incorporated in what was called 'Public Service Obligation'. The Government issued a statement that they 'did not envisage a substantial programme of closures and that they had decided to subsidise the rail passenger system as a whole'. The 1974 Railways Act was passed and this stated that 'The British Railways Board shall from 1 January 1975 operate their railway passenger system as to provide a public service which is *generally comparable at present.'* The word 'generally' did not, for example, stop the Bridport branch closing in May of that year. The Act wrote off a further £298 million of BR

losses (in addition to the hundreds of millions written off in previous years following the Modernisation Plan fiasco), effectively providing a financial clean slate from the beginning of 1975.

At the end of 1974 there were 100 loss-making services or groups of services that were being grant-aided under the provisions of the 1968 Transport Act, already described. These grant payments had escalated to £125 million. However, as a whole the railways continued to lose vast sums of money and between 1975 and 1982 between £522 million and £722 million was lost every year.

It could be argued that by the end of the 1970s the pace of closures had almost stopped, leading to a period of relative consolidation, but by that time so many branch and minor lines had been closed that there were only so many left on the closure list. In any event, the 1963 Beeching *Reshaping of British Railways* report was stated to be a 15-year plan and although there had been some changes in direction over the years the theoretical end date for the implementation of the report's recommendations would have been 1978, virtually the end of the decade.

◀ Another electrified branch line, albeit on the 1,500-volt dc system, was from Manchester Piccadilly to Glossop. This was the same system as employed on the entire Woodhead route from the early 1950s. The service was operated by Class 506 EMUs, which were introduced in 1954. Woodhead route passenger services ceased in 1970 and the line across the Pennines closed altogether in 1981. However, the Glossop line continued with dc services until re-equipped for ac working in 1984, whereupon the Class 506s were withdrawn. No M59408M arrives at Dinting on its way to Manchester in 1977. *Author*

▶ Another London Midland Region electrified branch line terminated at Croxley Green near Watford. When photographed on 11 March 1970 Class 501 units operated between London Euston and either Watford Junction via Watford High Street, or Croxley Green via Watford West. These units were withdrawn in May 1985. The line was 'temporarily' closed in 1996 when part of an embankment was removed during road improvement works, the station technically being kept 'open' by the use of replacement buses, an operational nonsense. Croxley Green station, seen here, will never reopen. *Author*

▲ The Lake District did not fare well in the Beeching-era cuts although, surprisingly, the Cumbrian Coast line did survive. Not so fortunate was the branch from Penrith to Keswick. The line beyond Keswick through Bassenthwaite Lake to Workington closed in April 1966 and in March 1972 it was the turn of the remaining Penrith to Keswick section. With signs of neglect everywhere to be seen this two-car DMU pauses at the commodious and architecturally attractive Keswick station in 1970. *Author*

◀ Penrith for Ullswater says the sign, referring to an area of the Lake District rather than a station on a branch line. The Keswick branch train, seen here in 1970, normally departed from Platform 4 beneath a slightly unusual roof arrangement. The bay platform is trackless, with the West Coast Main Line tracks out of frame on the right. Within a couple of years the branch line metals would be covered in rust. *Author*

◀ This delightful little branch goods headed by Class 25 Bo-Bo No 25060 is coming off the freight-only line to Sutton-in-Ashfield at Kirkby Summit signalbox on 19 June 1980. At this time the occasional freight served the Metal Box Company in the town. The Great Northern, Great Central and Midland railways all had a presence in this area, but the only survivor is the Robin Hood line from Nottingham to Worksop. *Author*

▲ By January 1978, the overall roof at Cromer station had been sealed off and the stop blocks had been relocated outside the old trainshed, thus ruining the atmosphere of the old station (see page 113). The goods yard had been ripped up and it would not be long before the BR Property Board found a buyer for the available land. All trains travelling to and from Sheringham reverse at Cromer, although there was once a direct spur that could have obviated this necessity. The Gloucester RC&W Company Class 100 DMU would soon be on its way. *Author*

▼ More rationalisation, but this time at Sudbury, Suffolk, at the end of the branch from Marks Tey. In times past passengers could have continued their journeys to either Bury St Edmunds or Cambridge, but by the time this view was recorded on 13 February 1982, those lines had been closed for many years. It seemed a tragedy to have such a fine GER station building boarded up, the weed-covered island platform trackless with not a creature comfort in sight, except for a bit of awning. No ticket office, no station staff, no warm waiting room, no toilet facilities, and not even a platform light. Some called it progress! *Author*

▲ Some people would say that the Cambrian Coast line is just one great big branch line, while others might argue that it was part of the Cambrian Railways' main line. However, having travelled the routes on many occasions it is possible to confirm that operations are commensurate with branch line practice in every respect. Hanging to the cliffs on a narrow ledge high above the Irish Sea is the 15.07 Pwllheli to Wolverhampton of 23 June 1979. The town of Fairbourne is visible in the left background. The attractive coastal line survived the ravages of the 1960s and 1970s and remains open. *Author*

▼ This photograph was published many years ago but it passed the editorial sift because of its rarity. Although the Class 35 'Hymek' diesel-hydraulics worked Class 1 express trains, particularly between South Wales and London, many were eventually 'put out to grass' and performed rather mundane duties on miscellaneous branch lines. Certainly there would be no 90mph running with the Newcastle Emlyn to Carmarthen goods, comprising three empty coal wagons and a brakevan. The wonderful ensemble is passing the closed Llandyssil station in 1970. The branch opened in July 1895, passenger services along the line ceased in September 1952, and freight finally ended in October 1973. *Author*

▲ The railway lines of the South Wales valleys have been decimated over the years, but passenger trains still run to Rhymney, Merthyr Tydfil, Aberdare, Treherbert and Maesteg, with Ebbw Vale recently added to the list. Since this photograph was taken in 1974, Merthyr Tydfil has been heavily rationalised and one will no longer find a 'mixed' train comprising a three-car DMU and parcels van waiting to leave for Cardiff General. The platform on the right no longer served any useful purpose, other than for photography! *Author*

▼ There is nothing quite like the world of slate that surrounds Blaenau Ffestiniog, especially when the train in the station is an interesting Chartex working. The Railway Pictorial Publications Railtours (RPPR) 'Conway Consort' special from Paddington on 7 October 1978 was hauled from Llandudno Junction by classes of locomotive that were nearing the end of their days on BR, Class 40 'Whistler' No 40113, seen here, and one of the last-surviving Class 24s, No 24082. It was great to travel on a full-length train over the 27¼-mile single-track branch. *Author*

▲ There is plenty of evidence in this photograph that the Ashford to Hastings line was double track until rationalisation reared its ugly head. Thumping along between Three Oaks and Doleham 3R 'Oxted' unit No 1306 is seen heading towards Ashford on 24 April 1981. Once the line was singled the only passing place between Ore and Appledore was at the ancient town of Rye. The line survives, but now it is Class 170 diesel units that operate under the 'Southern' marketing name. *Author*

◄ The preservation of the 1865 Mid-Hants Railway is another success story, even though only part of the line, from Alton to Alresford, could be saved. Having served as a diversionary route between Pirbright Junction and Winchester during the 1967 Bournemouth electrification scheme, the non-electrified line closed completely in February 1973. A year before closure, 3H unit No 1128 arrives at Alresford with an Alton to Southampton working. The signalman has crossed the line to effect a single-line token change with the driver, who is leaning from his cab. *Author*

◄ In this further Cambrian scene there is much to absorb at Talerddig, the summit of the long climb up from Machynlleth. The signalman has crossed the track from his signalbox and is waiting on his rostrum to gather the single-line token from the driver of Birmingham New Street-bound DMU No T313 on a wet day in July 1988. Note that both upper and lower quadrant signals are in operation. After 104 years of service the box was abolished shortly afterwards when radio-token signalling was introduced. Considerable further expenditure continues on new state-of-the-art signalling on Cambrian lines to improve timekeeping. *Author*

► It seems a recurring theme when reviewing our branch and minor lines during the BR years, that the most wonderful and historic structures were unnecessarily condemned for the want of some imagination regarding diversified use. The lovely little terminus of Henley-on-Thames looks forlorn and dilapidated in this 1972 photograph, whereas in GWR days one can be sure that the stationmaster took great pride in his station. If saving the cost of station staff wages and paint on buildings was designed to make BR profitable, the policy manifestly failed! The DMU will shortly leave for Twyford. *Author*

► One effect of mass line and station closures was the creation of a sizeable industry in railway relics and ephemera. While such items as locomotive nameplates and railway tickets have been collected for decades, the hobby expanded into many other areas and at auction some realised astronomical amounts. The old Minehead totem sign featured here would now command a four-figure sum at auction and by way of example many interesting station clocks would have a greater value. Even alloy diesel hydraulic nameplates now sell for thousands of pounds. The Minehead branch opened to Watchet in 1862 and to Minehead in 1874, but this view shows the Somerset terminus in 1970, the year before closure, with a DMU waiting to leave for Taunton. It is now the home of the West Somerset Railway (see page 121). *Author*

► There are no signal arms on the signal gantry, no wires on the telegraph posts, no track at three of the four platform faces, and no sidings remain. The scene is Exmouth on 3 January 1970 and it is clear that the days of the through seaside excursion are well and truly over. The Exmouth branch survives to this day, but the line to Budleigh Salterton and Sidmouth Junction closed in March 1967. This land was all sold off and now a single platform and a small modern station building are located on the west side of the site, right. The distant DMU will shortly depart for Exeter Central. *Author*

1980s AND SECTORISATION

EVER SINCE THE RAILWAYS WERE NATIONALISED there has been perpetual Government interference in their funding, running and organisation. The fundamental problem has always been that the railway system as a whole was loss-making. Losses have to be covered by borrowing or subsidy and the size of the business is so great that only a government could, realistically, fund the seemingly perpetual losses. With a railway network having its origins in the Victorian era, with trade unions that objected to just about every significant change in working practices or reduction in manpower (with a consequent loss of members), and with a Board that did not anticipate changes in the behaviour of the travelling public, the running of our railways has always been in the headlines. Report after report and guru after guru tried to turn the railways around so that vast annual losses were not continually funded by taxpayers, who increasingly became car owners with little interest in the state of the railways, but who had a great interest in their tax bills.

The problem seemed insoluble as even the implementation of hundreds of draconian measures and recommendations contained in various reviews and Transport Acts, including those in the very profound reshaping report, the railways still lost money. Towards the end of 1982 under the Conservative Thatcher Government the Secretary of State for Transport, the Rt Hon. David Howell MP, was encouraged to instigate yet another review to examine railway finances rather than transport policy. The terms of reference were hardly concise: 'To examine the finances of the railway and associated operations, in the light of all relevant considerations, and to report on options for alternative policies, and their related objectives, designed to secure improved financial results in an efficiently run railway in Great Britain over the next 20 years.' The chairman of the review was to be Sir David Serpell, a senior civil servant and former Permanent Secretary, who in past years had worked with Lord Beeching.

By 1982, BR was again in an awful mess financially. Gross receipts amounted to £1,692 million while costs amounted to £2,477 million. The Public Service Obligation Grant (PSO) was £809 million. The business carried 2 million passengers per day Monday to Friday and 1,900 goods trains ran daily. However, the railways were carrying only 54 per cent of the amount of freight carried in 1950. During the same period passenger rail travel decreased but only marginally. There were about 200,000 employees, including British Rail Engineering Ltd. Unfortunately, a series of industrial disputes in 1982 had cost the industry some £140 million

and the Government's patience was understandably wearing thin. By this time the total wage bill was already 60 per cent of its total expenditure and higher wages would simply and directly inflate the losses being made.

At the time Serpell was considering all the issues for his report, the early stages of sectorisation had been implemented. Replacing the old regional structures new business groups had been created with passenger services falling within the categories of InterCity (IC), Network SouthEast (NSE), and Provincial (Regional Railways). Other sectors included Railfreight and Parcels. Provincial services included cross-country and city regional trains, long and short branch lines, and stopping services on many main lines. In pure profit-and-loss terms IC and NSE were in the credit column of the balance sheet, but the position regarding Provincial was dire. The sector accounted for 75 per cent of all passenger revenues but on the whole, loading factors were a miserable 20 per cent of capacity. That sector alone was losing £104 million per annum, far more than any profit made by the other sectors.

The report singled out the Leamington Spa to Stratford-upon-Avon service where annual receipts of £76,000 compared very unfavourably with direct costs of £425,000! Serpell and his colleagues, supported by consultants, described the Provincial sector as 'poor value for money' pointing out that guaranteed and subsidised buses could provide a substitute for many of these rail services with a major saving to the public purse. The startling fact was that every passenger journey throughout the year on Provincial was subsidised by the taxpayer to the tune of 22.6p per mile! The report also confirmed that the amount of money spent on track maintenance was divided into four categories, depending upon usage, line speed and loading factors, but suggested that standards 'might well be reduced on minor lines', thereby saving money.

Some commentators of the day and many MPs said that the 1983 Serpell report exceeded its terms of reference in that some recommendations were policy issues rather than financial aspects. For example, it was recommended that all double-track rail routes should be singled if there were less than 10,000 train movements per annum (about 34 trains per day based on a six-day week). As regards further line closures the report stated that 'the withdrawal of all loss-making services (except certain London commuter services) was an option except where the resource cost of withdrawing the service would be greater than that of retaining it'. However, the primary thrust of the report was

▲ There are a large number of freight-only branch lines that are in effect lengthy sidings, often to industrial installations. All contribute to railway income by providing feeder traffic to the national network. A good example is at Earles Sidings near Hope in Derbyshire where a single-track branch runs down to the Lafarge (formerly Blue Circle) cement works. In June 1983, Class 08 shunter No 08543 heads some massive, loaded cement bogie wagons towards Earles Sidings where there will be an interchange with the cross-Pennine Hope Valley route. *Author*

▼ Many years ago this Class 40 could have been heading south for Ashbourne and Uttoxeter along the Tissington Trail, but when photographed on 23 March 1982 it would have been travelling light to quarry sidings at either Hindlow or Dowlow to collect a load of stone or lime. The drystone walls and magnificent hills surround the spa town of Buxton, visible in the distance. No 40094 was withdrawn seven months later, in October 1982. The line is still open for freight. The passenger service over this route closed as long ago as November 1954. *Author*

to provide a number of (somewhat controversial) options, which to be fair, were mentioned in the original terms of reference. The most radical of these was to reduce the railway network by a whopping 84 per cent, leaving just 1,630 miles of main line, with obviously every secondary and branch line being closed. This was the only one of six options which would result in an operating profit.

Another option was for a 2,200-mile network, incurring a small loss. Other options proposed route miles of between 15,300 and 17,200 with various line configurations but where quite substantial subsidies would be required to cover losses. The summary of these options was fairly obvious to the student of railways: 'It is clear to us that reductions in the size of the network will be required if the level of financial support for the railway is to be lowered substantially.'

One of the consultants on the Serpell Committee did not agree with the conclusions of many of his colleagues. Alfred Goldstein produced his own minority report. There is not the space here to detail all his observations but his paper included two splendid quotes that to the author, adequately describe the British public psyche towards railways and the seemingly irrefutable fact that railway networks do not make a profit. His comments are recorded verbatim:

a. 'The attachment many of us have for the present railway is not reflected in the fares we are prepared to pay, since these fares do not reflect the full cost.'

b. 'The real issue is what size and quality of railway should the nation decide to support having regard to the many demands on taxpayer's money.'

Unfortunately for Serpell, the production of a minority report diluted the committee's findings. Also, although the report was comprehensive and lengthy, insufficient time was allowed for the committee to delve deeply into some of the supporting data, thereby losing credibility. Furthermore, even though the committee had been requested to provide options, the public and the press focussed only on his radical Option A, which was the tiny, 1,630-mile system, a sort of 'super Beeching' approach, and all the headlines were negative. The most charitable comment was that Option A was 'a valuable illustration but not a practical option'.

The Chairman of the British Railways Board described Serpell personally as being 'as cosy as a razor blade'! In Parliament Serpell's options were described as 'unrealistic to the point of madness'. Another said that 'Serpell was pessimism seeking to wear the clothes of realism.' A member of the opposition stated 'that this house opposes massive rail network cuts and commuter fare increases, and condemns the government for its failure to reject outright the Serpell Report'. In the event, the report was shelved, the episode ended David Howell's ministerial career, and even more public money was wasted on the report's preparation. Sir David Serpell died in 2008 aged 96.

Having set up the BR sectors in an effort to make the railway more accountable by the use of profit centres with delegated management responsibility for everything from performance to finance, in marketing terms the railways of Britain changed shape in the 1980s. New train liveries appeared, station signs were changed and the motive power on many of our branch and minor lines was changing, as many of the 30-year-old diesel mechanical multiple units were replaced by more modern stock, featuring sliding doors, public address systems and increased performance. During the 1980s it seemed as if there was an attack on infrastructure in that numerous station buildings were demolished, hundreds of 'bus shelters' started to grace the platforms of minor stations and halts, there was a relentless attack on semaphore signalling and signalboxes, as well as the removal of all surplus track and sidings, some of it a leftover from the days of steam and locomotive run-rounds. One of the gainers was the BR Property Board, as everything from large tracts of redundant land to some 'des res' station buildings were sold off for considerable sums. In city areas millions of pounds changed hands, before a property recession occurred at the end of the decade.

Goods yards everywhere had given over to car parks with, sadly, the income generated at many sites considerably exceeding any income generated by a wagon or two from the occasional pick-up goods train. Even the railway relics of yesteryear were generating cash as enthusiasts flooded into BR's Collectors Corner to purchase some keepsake from the past. Diesel locomotive nameplates were sold off with values appreciating rapidly. Nevertheless, in operational terms the average passenger fare for all types of rail ticket was 5.3p per mile and yet the public subsidies to the railways was 5.4p per mile and so whatever grants, subsidies or other dodges were employed, the fact was that the BR system was continuing to lose vast sums of money, and the Government was continuing to try to find a way out of supporting the railway business.

Although there were few passenger line closures in the 1980s the same could not be said for freight-only branches. As a result of the suicidal miners' dispute in the mid-1980s, when again the railways lost income through industrial disputes, many uneconomic pits were closed and this in itself resulted in railway line closures. Other industries also declined and many of these had their own dedicated branch lines or lengthy sidings. Some of these formerly had a passenger service while others had always been freight only. A small sample of lines that disappeared from the railway map in the 1980s were the line to New Holland Pier, Sheffield (Wath Road Junction) to Leeds (Goose Hill Junction), March to Spalding, Huddersfield (Shepley) to Clayton West, Woodside to Sanderstead, Bedford St John's, Tunbridge Wells to Eridge, the line to Broad Street (London), and amongst over 300 freight lines and spurs closed in the decade, the little Carbis Wharf branch in Cornwall finally succumbed in 1989.

▲ The headboard on the front of Brush/Sulzer Type 4 No 47258 reads '1872–1989, Watlington Branch – Last BR Train'. The last passenger train had run from Princes Risborough to Watlington in July 1957, but since that date the main source of traffic had been coal deliveries to the Rugby cement works at Chinnor. In December 1989 this traffic ceased and here we see the last train of empty vacuum-braked hopper wagons. The Chinnor & Princes Risborough Railway now operates over 3½ miles of track, with the objective of connecting with the national network at Princes Risborough. *Author*

▼ This photograph should be compared with that on page 145 depicting Henley-on-Thames station and the sentiment contained in the caption noted. By February 1982 the old station at Henley-on-Thames had been officially vandalised as the quest for income from railway property started to rival Victorian railwaymania. Selling truly redundant land is of course justified, but it was hardly in the interests of the rail traveller where land was sold off for redevelopment and whole stations were moved further away from towns. A most unusual visitor is featured in the shape of six-car 'Hastings' DEMU No 1031, which was chartered by the Branch Line Society for a tour of London branches. *Author*

By the end of the decade the closure mentality had virtually disappeared, road congestion was on the agenda and green credentials were in fashion, but it was all too late for many minor railway lines. The Provincial or Regional Railways lines continued to lose money and for the Government the following decade would see determined efforts to move British Rail(ways) down the road towards privatisation.

The subject of closure dates is not straightforward. Throughout this book most closure dates quoted refer to the Monday following the last weekend of service, whether there was a Saturday and Sunday service or not. Sometimes a last-day railway enthusiasts' Chartex special ran after the last timetabled service train. However, in many cases lines remained open for freight traffic and the inclusion of the words 'closed to passengers' often inferred that in many cases goods traffic continued to operate over all or part of the former passenger line. Another problem regarding precise closure dates arose with freight-only branches because the published closure date was in many cases many months after the last train actually ran.

Another category of closure complicated the issue because lines could be taken out of use, which obviously meant that they were not necessarily closed, but could no longer be used, without perhaps the reinstatement of a point or a length of track. This particularly applied to mothballed lines, where it was anticipated they could possibly be reopened at a later date. In a handful of cases lines were officially closed but then briefly reopened for one reason or another. In a few cases the closure date is simply not known. Some enthusiasts take great pleasure in recording closure dates as accurately as possible, while others are content to know that a line closed in a certain year. In this tome the published closure dates used have been from reliable sources but for the reasons stated, some of these dates can be somewhat wayward.

Although there has always been heated discussions about the first standard-gauge line to be preserved, well-established names such as the Bluebell Railway and the Middleton Railway were both at the forefront of railway preservation in one way or another in the 1950s and early '60s. However, prior to the 1950s there were no preserved working railways as we know them today, and it was the Welsh narrow-gauge fans who led the field in saving some of our heritage in terms of operational lines. The Stephenson Locomotive Society had been active in standard-gauge locomotive preservation back in 1927 and the railway companies themselves had saved some significant locomotives and vehicles. Many other preservation societies joined the movement in the 1960s and it was the closures of the late 1960s, '70s and '80s that provided the greatest opportunities for preserving branch lines or sections of minor lines. While a few schemes fell by the wayside over 60 have subsequently flourished, a bonus of the Beeching report recommendations and subsequent closures perhaps?

▼ Over the years, all the old Great Eastern Railway branch lines between London and Ipswich have been electrified with the exception of Sudbury. Similarly in terms of suburban services out of Liverpool Street all branches have been electrified including the Enfield Town branch seen here. The station enjoys a half-hourly service to Liverpool Street, and Class 315 No 315837 waits to leave with such a working in January 1987. All the modern diesel and electric units have sliding doors, the last slam-door branch line stock being used on the Lymington branch in Hampshire until May 2010. *Author*

▶ Here, in December 1989, we see something of an anachronism of a diesel unit working on an electrified GER branch line. Ex-Sudbury Network SouthEast Class 101 DMU No L220 has just arrived under the wires at its destination of Colchester St Botolph's station, which is now called Colchester Town. Care has been taken to include both St Botolph's Church and St Botolph's station in the photograph! The older-generation DMUs would soon disappear from the scene and on the next visit to Sudbury, a Class 156 DMU was working the branch. *Author*

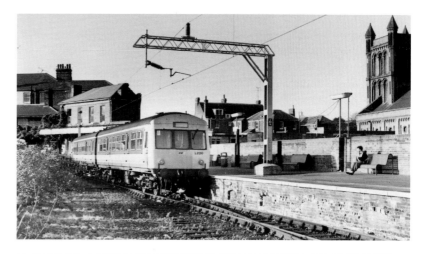

▶ There can be few train units that are as unattractive as this SR style of 2-EPB (electro-pneumatic brake) EMU, latterly designated Class 416/3. Even though these units were refurbished in the early 1980s at Eastleigh and Horwich works, they still rode heavily, retained their multiple draft-inducing doors and imprisoned passengers with bars at the windows, a safety feature for some of the lines they travelled over. All have been withdrawn. When combined with the trackside litter strewn by an ignorant minority and the local yobbo putting his wet feet where others might care to sit, this January 1987 scene at the now-abandoned North Woolwich terminus makes one appreciate the country branch line! No 6315 will shortly depart for Richmond. *Author*

▶ A seaside terminus, semaphore signalling, a class of locomotive that was then near the end of its career, and you have an irresistible combination. Arriving at Skegness in September 1984 is English Electric Class 40 'Whistler' No 40181 with hundreds of railfans cramming the leading coaches and flailing from the windows. The front coaches were of course nearest the locomotive and where English Electric exhaust sounds were at their best. Although under the Beeching proposals the line would have closed, a 21st-century decision was taken to invest heavily in the line, particularly on track renewal programmes. Note the ornate barge boards on the signalbox. *Author*

▲ This smashing little branch freight is seen trundling along the north-west end of the Severn Valley line from Bridgnorth. When photographed in May 1988 the remaining stub of the line from Sutton Bridge Junction, Shrewsbury served a fuel depot at Shrewsbury Abbey, terminus of the old Shropshire & Montgomeryshire Railway. On this day, the Class 08 shunter had but a single wagon to collect. Needless to say, the line closed shortly afterwards, on 5 July 1988. The photographer was in the nick of time before the national network rail map was, unfortunately, further reduced in size. *Author*

▼ In many parts of the country attractive and interesting branch lines served only industry, some of them having always been 'freight-only' while others were former passenger lines that had been retained as freight-only lines, sometimes for decades after the passenger services had ceased. Such was the case at Markham Colliery sidings on 10 June 1980 as a single Class 20, No 20210, arrived from the Bolsover Colliery direction with hoppers. Between the locomotive and the lovely Midland Railway signalbox the signalman waits for the single-line token, while behind him are slag heaps of waste from the mining industry. These Derbyshire collieries both closed in 1993; at the time the Government announced that they were 'testing the financial impact of not cutting coal'! *Author*

▲ In some areas there is a branch line off a branch line, but in this case it was a siding off a freight-only line. Just north of what, in November 1987 was the passenger railhead of Aylesbury there was once a Peakstone terminal and a Cawood coal depot, both extending from the former Metropolitan & Great Central Joint line, by then freight only to Quainton Road and Calvert. A new Railfreight-liveried Class 56 was having its stone train unloaded at the site, while an engineers' crane occupied the other siding. The new Aylesbury Vale Parkway station was opened in this vicinity in December 2008. *Author*

▼ Further north from the Aylesbury site is Calvert, on the former Great Central Railway main line, which closed to passengers in September 1966, being considered a duplicate route from the East Midlands into London. Passing the old, abandoned island platform on 14 November 1987, on what by then was very much a branch line, 1,470hp Class 31 No 31127 was heading the weekly UK Fertiliser Company train of empties from Akeman Street to Ince & Elton. In the background is the Greater London Council waste disposal terminal. *Author*

▲ At Crianlarich in Perthshire, the Caledonian Railway line to Oban met the North British Railway route to the West Highlands and where each line once had its own station. As with the Cambrian, these routes were substantially single track and resembled branch lines even though they were also main lines, there being a King's Cross to Fort William through train. With the Fort William line visible just to the left of the cab of this Class 37, No 37405 leaves Crianlarich for Oban in November 1986. Both lines survive. *Author*

▼ Warcop station in the old county of Westmorland was on the North Eastern Railway Stainmore route from Penrith to Darlington via Kirkby Stephen and Barnard Castle. It closed to passenger services west of Barnard Castle in January 1962 and east thereof in November 1964. By 26 March 1982, only the stub from Appleby to Warcop remained in use, mainly by the Army for freight traffic. Framed between leafless trees Class 26 No 26028 nears Warcop with just a single four-wheel munitions wagon in tow. The line was closed and mothballed on 20 May 1987 and since then, the Eden Valley Railway has moved in, operating trains from 2002. *Author*

▲ More railway architecture desecration, but this time at Ilkley station in West Yorkshire, which opened in 1865. This immensely attractive building was where the Midland Railway and the North Eastern Railway (Otley & Ilkley Joint) shared services. Platforms 3 and 4 on the right served the line to Skipton via the now-preserved Bolton Abbey–Embsay section, which closed to BR passengers in 1965. The space between the platforms was subsequently filled in and converted to a car park and in the late 1980s a supermarket was built underneath the all-over roof section, with the surviving platforms being shortened. The lines to Bradford and Leeds were electrified in 1995, becoming the Wharfedale Lines but on this June day in 1986 it was a humble two-car DMU that was about to leave for Bradford (Forster Square). *Author*

▼ It was not only stations that the railway builders of the Victorian age built on a grand scale. Goods and transfer sheds could also be impressive and in retrospect, especially when viewed after closure, somewhat oversized. However, old photographs show scores of wagons in some of the sidings and no doubt when built the volume of traffic and size of shed were related. This substantial stone building was located at Clayton West, the terminus of a branch from Shepley on the Huddersfield to Penistone line. In this image, recorded shortly before closure in January 1983, a five-car DMU stands at the platform. The 15in-gauge Kirklees Light Railway now runs over part of the old branch. *Author*

◄ With due respect to the railway engineers, it would appear from the rotting timbers visible in this photograph that there was a risk of this Class 108 DMU falling into the River Humber! With every timber in sight needing either paint or preservative the end is nigh for passenger services at New Holland Pier, a spur off the Barton-upon-Humber branch line in north Lincolnshire. Before the opening of the road suspension bridge across the River Humber ferries would ply across the river from this point. This photograph was taken on 12 June 1981, two weeks before the line closed and the bridge opened. *Gavin Morrison*

◄◣ The station of Colne on the line from Accrington via Rose Grove was on the old Lancashire & Yorkshire Railway, but the route further north through to Skipton was Midland Railway territory. Colne became a passenger terminus in February 1970 when the service to Skipton was discontinued. Goods services were also axed and the line lifted. This grey and blue Class 108 DMU is ready to leave with the 12.46 to Preston on 10 November 1982. The station 'building', right of cab, is not L&YR! *Gavin Morrison*

◄▼ Few enthusiasts would have thought that they would ever go exploring branch lines by High Speed Train, but that is precisely what happened on 18 February 1990. Hertfordshire Railtours ran a special to the end of the Wensleydale branch, then served only by freight workings to the Tarmac depot at Redmire. The line once continued through to Garsdale, but passenger services ceased in the 1950s. The power cars are Nos 43013 and 43014, and above the nearest car is Bolton Castle that dates back to 1399 and is situated in the Yorkshire Dales National Park. *Gavin Morrison*

▼ In this most unusual impression of Oban station, Class 37 No 37175 is heading tank wagons off the MWFO 7B05 Mossend to Oban on 2 May 1984. There are some empties for the back run behind the splendid Austin Princess limousine on the right. Sadly, out of the 309 delivered, only a handful of these purposeful Type 3 1,750hp locomotives remain in main line service but at least this example is now preserved, privately owned, on Scottish Railway Preservation Society property at Bo'ness. It has not always worked in Scotland and in 1986 was transferred to work china clay trains in Cornwall before later returning north. *Gavin Morrison*

▲ This cheerful welcoming sign adorns the all-over roof at the most distant location from London on the entire BR network, Wick station. For many years an additional locomotive to the train engine was required at this northern outpost to handle both Wick and Thurso portions of trains arriving at Georgemas Junction from Inverness. On 30 June 1987, No 37420 *The Scottish Hosteller* is ready to leave with the Wick portion of the 12.00 departure for Inverness. *Gavin Morrison*

▼ With the remains of the winter snows on the top of the hills this Scottish 'Duff', Class 47/4 No 47460, with snowploughs and headboard, ducks under the power lines as it leaves Dufftown (!) with an InterCity land cruise, returning to the junction at Keith, between Aberdeen and Inverness. Beyond Dufftown the line once continued to Craigellachie and then to either Elgin (closed 1968) or via the Speyside line to Aviemore (closed 1965). *Gavin Morrison*

▲ Strange operational arrangements still occur at Ormskirk, seen here, and at Kirby in the north Merseyside area, where end-on connections are made between electrified and non-electrified lines. At Ormskirk there is, however, an emergency connection, seen here on the right, which is of course, rarely used. A Class 108 DMU from Preston (left) meets a Class 507 EMU from Liverpool (right) on 23 May 1983. The former line is largely single track. *Gavin Morrison*

▼ Depicted here is a Merseyside electric scene before the old Class 503 EMUs were withdrawn during 1985. The class had its origins in the LMS before the Second World War and the main tranches were delivered in 1938 and 1956. Doors in the centre of each driving cab were fitted from 1972 as a safety requirement. At the end of the New Brighton branch on the Wirral peninsular Nos M29279M and M28394M in blue and grey livery are seen at the terminus on 28 April 1983. *Gavin Morrison*

▲ In this lower Welsh valleys scene at Taffs Well, both operational and mothballed double-track branch lines can be seen. With lower quadrant signals controlling the scene diesel units between Cardiff Central and Treherbert, Aberdare and Merthyr Tydfil ply backwards and forwards, in total several times per hour. The unit with the Welsh dragon on the back is Treherbert bound while the Class 101, without indicator blind, is heading for Radyr and Cardiff, in September 1986. The fully signalled but abandoned lines to the right are part of the old Rhymney Railway route to the Caerphilly area where connections were made with several other routes. *Author*

▼ A mere quarter of a century ago, on 18 September 1986, a timeless scene such as this was still possible to photograph. A good old diesel mechanical unit, No C302, forming the 11.30 from Barry Island to Merthyr Tydfil, prepares to cross over to the platform road at Abercynon, while the signalman stands on the platform end to exchange tokens. The magnificent and permanent-looking signalbox and the handsome signal gantry are dwarfed by the surrounding hillsides, all in all a delightful branch line scene. *Author*

▲ Using the signalbox as a vantage point this was the view of Barry Island station in September 1986. The station had seen much better times and was looking tired, but not derelict. Before the Second World War huge numbers of excursionists used the line to visit the adjacent pleasure grounds. A three-car DMU waits for departure for one of the valley lines, destination unrecorded. To the left of this view was Dai Woodham's scrapyard where scores of steam locomotives were dumped and cut up, but also where many were subsequently purchased for preservation. The line beyond ran through a tunnel to Barry Pier for a connection to Severn Estuary steamers. The line was opened in 1899 and abandoned in 1976. *Author*

▼ More lower quadrant semaphore signals in the South Wales valleys but this time at Ystrad Mynach. DMU set No C334, complete with red Welsh dragon on the cab end, arrives at the station with a train from Merthyr Tydfil to Penarth in September 1986. The line diverging to the left was to Penallta Colliery, while the line to Cwm Bargoed is at a higher level, out of sight at upper left, where occasional coal trains still run. In years gone by the route afforded access to numerous branch lines and collieries. *Author*

▲ This symmetrical line-up of upper quadrant semaphore signals survived at Tunbridge Wells West until closure of the lines to Eridge and Tunbridge Wells Central in July 1985. Arriving at the old LBSCR station in this famous spa town during April 1985, is 'Oxted' three-car DEMU No 1314. Long after closure the Spa Valley Railway commenced operations, having secured the line to Groombridge with eventual extension to Eridge on the national rail network in 2011. *Author*

▼ Looking at the erstwhile Southern Region route map the non-electrified line from Hurst Green south of Oxted to Uckfield is a surviving anachronism, rivalled only by the Ore to Ashford route. The reliable English Electric 3D, 3H and 3R DEMUs operated the Uckfield service for over 40 years until they were pensioned off in 2003 and new-generation Class 170s were introduced. This Class 205 unit in Network SouthEast livery is seen approaching Birchden Junction in January 1989 on a service from Uckfield. *Author*

▶ This closure notice, with white and black printing on a green background appeared in the waiting room at Tunbridge Wells West station three months before actual closure. The notice somewhat formally quoted the relevant legislation but few passengers would have ever heard of either Grove Junction or Birchden Junction. The bold print contained the dreaded news and the rest of the text would have been largely irrelevant. After closure, inhabitants of the town and rail travellers would still be able to reach the outside world but from Tunbridge Wells Central station on the Tonbridge to Hastings line. *Author*

▼ In days gone by Eridge station was a true junction with rail routes to Polegate via Hailsham, Brighton via Uckfield, Tonbridge via Tunbridge Wells West, London via Oxted and, theoretically, Three Bridges via East Grinstead. However, when photographed in November 1986 and despite the busy-looking track configuration, only the Hurst Green to Uckfield route was open. The signalbox was later abolished, the signals felled and only a single line was operational through the station. Happily the public house by the station remained open throughout! DEMU No 205018 departs for Oxted. *Author*

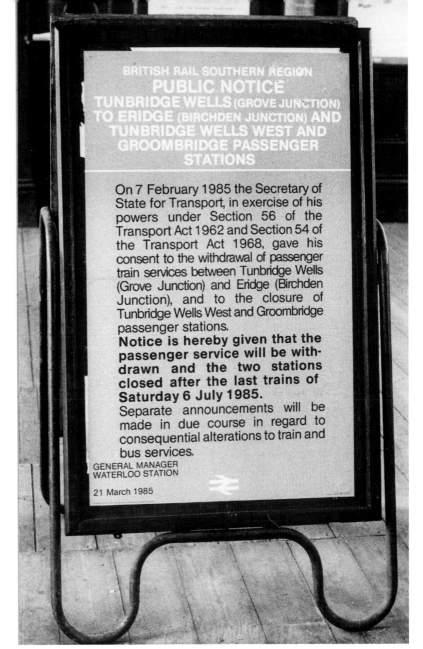

BRITISH RAIL SOUTHERN REGION
PUBLIC NOTICE
**TUNBRIDGE WELLS (GROVE JUNCTION)
TO ERIDGE (BIRCHDEN JUNCTION) AND
TUNBRIDGE WELLS WEST AND
GROOMBRIDGE PASSENGER
STATIONS**

On 7 February 1985 the Secretary of State for Transport, in exercise of his powers under Section 56 of the Transport Act 1962 and Section 54 of the Transport Act 1968, gave his consent to the withdrawal of passenger train services between Tunbridge Wells (Grove Junction) and Eridge (Birchden Junction), and to the closure of Tunbridge Wells West and Groombridge passenger stations.
Notice is hereby given that the passenger service will be withdrawn and the two stations closed after the last trains of Saturday 6 July 1985.
Separate announcements will be made in due course in regard to consequential alterations to train and bus services.
GENERAL MANAGER
WATERLOO STATION

21 March 1985

▲ Although there is no doubt that the line from Barnham (Junction) to Bognor Regis started life as a branch line with dedicated branch trains, it was not long before through coaches to London used the line. Since the late 1930s the double-track electrified line has had a very frequent service of four trains an hour to Littlehampton, Barnham and London Victoria, with extras at peak times. An unusual visitor in August 1989 was Class 73 No 73101 *Brighton Evening Argus* with the 'Venice Simplon Orient Express' Pullman set, seen just south of Barnham. The semaphore signals have since been removed. *Author*

▼ In this view just south of Lavant, the old LBSCR line from Chichester to Midhurst ran along the top of the embankment in the left background. Passenger services ceased in 1935, but general goods traffic to Lavant continued until 1968 and 1970 for sugar beet. The line was mothballed, but an aggregate terminal on a new alignment was ready for service in 1978. Aggregate trains shuttled between here and Drayton, Chichester, until 1991 when they ceased and the track was ripped up. Class 73s were the usual power, but on this day in February 1988, it was Class 33 'Crompton' No 33010 that was rostered. The trackbed is now a foot and cycle path from Fishbourne. *Author*

▲ The history of the Littlehampton branch is outlined on page 22 and the general story is broadly similar to the Bognor Regis branch, described opposite. Four electric trains per hour depart for Portsmouth, Bognor Regis and London but due to inept planning by TOC Southern, passengers for Brighton are now inconvenienced by having to change at Hove, except during peak periods when there are a handful of through trains. In this photograph, a train from London Victoria is arriving at the terminus in November 1984. At the time of writing semaphore signalling survives, but the old goods shed in the background has been demolished. *Author*

▼ The Seaford branch in East Sussex is one of contrasts. The initially double-track line passes through a river valley, a compact dockland area at Newhaven, along a shingle beach on a single line, and through a chalk cutting to a small seaside town. The line from Lewes to Newhaven opened in 1847 but it would be 1864 before it was extended eastward to Seaford. The extension was double track until singled in 1975. Approaching the intermediate station of Bishopstone in April 1985 is 4-CIG Class 423 unit No 7366 with a train from Brighton. Just visible, far right, are the platforms of Bishopstone Beach Halt (formerly Bishopstone Halt and before that, Bishopstone) which closed in 1942. The town of Newhaven forms the backdrop. *Author*

▲ Another scene beside the sea, although in this case it is the large Poole Harbour inlet. The location is Hamworthy Goods in Dorset, the end of a branch from Hamworthy (Junction), 116 miles from London on the Bournemouth to Weymouth route. The line is sought after on the itinerary of railway enthusiast special trains and on 19 March 1983 it was Hertfordshire Railtours and their 'Thames Piddle Executive' comprising two six-car 'Hastings' units, Nos 1032 and 1017, that visited the site. Never have more heads appeared from the windows of a train in the UK! *Author*

▼ Although already featured in the steam era, a photograph of the 'Channel Islands Boat Train' passing through the streets of Weymouth to Weymouth Quay at a walking pace and preceded by a railwayman with a warning hand bell was irresistible. On 22 October 1983, Class 33/1 No 33112 was diagrammed for the train of Mark 1 coaches from Waterloo. Often, railmen and the police had to bounce parked cars out of the way of the train before it could proceed, errant motorists thinking that this was some old disused dock line. The last service train ran in 1987, the last special in 1999 and as Network Rail had no further use for the line they sold it to the local authority for a token £50,000 in 2009, the end of an era that had started in 1865. *Author*

▲ Another surviving branch of great interest runs from Totton to Fawley in Hampshire, with an intermediate MoD siding and depot at Marchwood. For half a century the line had been heavily used by oil trains from the massive refinery at Fawley but underground pipelines now cover the country leaving only a modicum of rail traffic. Adding to the freight volumes, Railfreight Class 47 No 47256 leaves the military siding at Marchwood and makes for the main line in October 1989. Passenger services ceased in 1966, but the line is a possible candidate for passenger train reinstatement (see page 209). *Author*

▼ These old gates once 'protected' the MoD siding at Marchwood from the outside world, but now huge metal gates (behind the photographer) perform the task more efficiently. Regular military trains run from Didcot via Eastleigh Yard. On 5 November 1988 a rare visitor traversed the Fawley branch line in the shape of 'Peak' Class 45/1 No 45106 on Pathfinder Tours' 'Wessex Adventurer' special. There are still manual crossing gates and semaphore signals at Marchwood, a great attraction in this day and age. Note the signal 'dummy' and catch points that control entry to the main branch. *Author*

▲ After the Yatton to Witham via Wells branch line closed to passengers in 1963 goods traffic through to Cheddar via Cranmore carried on until 1969. Bitumen traffic from Ellesmere Port continued to be delivered to a depot at Cranmore in Somerset but this too ceased in September 1985. In the meantime, the East Somerset Railway had become established at Cranmore and on 25 May 1984 they required over 165 tons of ballast for track renewal, which was duly delivered by their Foster Yeoman near neighbours, in five Procor hopper wagons. The wagons were attached to the bitumen train seen here arriving behind No 47226. *Author*

▼ Few would have thought that these redundant Swindon-built china clay hood wagons would have ended their days in 1988 at Sharpness Docks beside the River Severn, just visible in the background. The wagons were tripped from St Blazey in dedicated trains over several weeks. Despite their appearance these vacuum-braked, wooden-sided wagons were built as recently as 1954–60 but based on much older designs. Passenger services along the branch from here to Berkeley Road station ceased in November 1964 and the only recent traffic has been to the now-closed Berkeley Nuclear Power Station. *Author*

▲ There was once a GWR line from Frome to Bristol via Radstock, where it was crossed by the Somerset & Dorset Railway, but the branch closed to passengers in November 1959. When photographed in 1980 the line from Frome ran only to the Marcroft wagon works at Radstock, but with an important intermediate siding that ran from Hapsford (Whatley Quarry Junction) to ARC's Whatley Quarry. The line from Hapsford, seen here, to Radstock West closed to freight on 29 June 1988 and scenes such as this were no more. No 47060 shunts some old wagons being loaded with sleepers from earlier track lifting. *Author*

▼ Although the Severn Beach branch has already been featured (see page 123) this view shows the almost complete isolation of the sterile terminus site. With not a human in sight and substantially devoid of platform lighting or shelter, the scene on 6 February 1982 was particularly bleak. SPC No W55033 waits for custom before returning to Bristol Temple Meads via Avonmouth. The line in the foreground once continued across the adjacent road to Pilning. Happily the branch survived and is now being actively promoted. *Author*

◀ By the late 1970s, BR was looking for new low-cost solutions for small lightweight diesel units to operate over lightly used lines. To some extent the then recent practices of the bus industry were adopted, certainly in terms of bodywork, which was Leyland National based. The engines were also from Leyland. The rest of the vehicles were of heavier 'railway' construction, including cab ends and four-wheel frame/chassis. The result was the 'Pacer' prototype or Class 140. No 140001 is seen at Calstock on the Gunnislake branch with the 14.45 to Plymouth on 3 July 1981. *Author*

◀ There is always room for humour on the railway scene and it came in abundance on the last ever RPPR railtour, the 'Mayflower' that ran on 12 October 1980. The main train was hauled by a Class 50 'Hoover' from Paddington to Newton Abbot where participants changed to a five-car DMU formation to visit several branch lines. Photographed at Heathfield, then the limit of the old Moretonhampstead branch, the driver seems bemused at the novel headboards, and that is before he had noted his destination was shown to be Windsor & Eton! The line curving away at top right was the Teign Valley line to Exeter St Thomas via Trusham, which closed in June 1958. *Author*

▲ Class 08 No 08953 creeps down the single track from Marsh Mills to Tavistock Junction with four loaded 80-ton Polybulk wagons from the nearby English China Clay works, just visible at top centre. Note the old Marsh Mills station platform on the left. The route was once part of the Plymouth to Launceston branch line, which closed to passengers in December 1962. Marsh Mills works has now closed to rail traffic, rendering this 1857 line redundant. Just around the corner to the left is the home of the Plym Valley Railway where trains run over a mile of track on several days a year. *Author*

▼ The alignment here at Yeoford appears to be double track with a freight running 'wrong line'. However, long after the Crediton to Okehampton passenger service ceased in 1972 the Barnstaple and Meldon Quarry (Okehampton) routes were both singled at this point resulting in two single-track lines running parallel. In August 1989, a 'Slim Jim' Class 33/2 nears Yeoford with loaded 'Seacow' wagons from Meldon. The routes combine at nearby Crediton. *Author*

◀ Signalboxes come in all shapes and sizes and this remarkable, elevated example is located high up on a cutting south of Ystrad Mynach on the old Rhymney Railway branch line to Cardiff. Note the incredible external staircase, the rollers and wires for the signals and the levers and rods for the points in this 1986 picture. Such infrastructure is forever diminishing, which should be savoured while still possible. *Author*

▼ Emerging from the cutting where the elevated Ystrad Mynach signalbox is located, and having diverged from the Rhymney branch, a brace of Class 37s with a rake of empty HAA coal hoppers from Aberthaw Power Station in tow, climb sharply towards either Nelson & Llancaiach, Taff Merthyr or Deep Navigation collieries, or Cwm Bargoed loading point. The staggered up platform and the two tracks on the left belong to the surviving Rhymney branch, as seen in September 1986. The Class 37s have long since disappeared from the Welsh valleys. *Author*

▲ Although slightly off the beaten track and now a mere shadow of its former self, the railway network at Burrows sidings near Swansea Docks was well worth a visit in April 1989. There were still industrial installations and therefore freight sidings and spurs in the area with a certainty of observing rail movement. Although still open, rail traffic has now decreased in the area. Leaving the yard with an articulated Cargowaggon is Class 08 No 08780. Top left are the oil storage tanks at BP Landarcy, south of the Neath to Swansea main line. *Author*

▶ A double-track branch line that was electrified back in 1987 runs from Oxted and Hurst Green to East Grinstead. The line once continued over what became the Bluebell Railway to Lewes with some services working through to Brighton. The branch was the last line to arrive in the town in 1884 and it is the last to survive (see also page 97). A handful of trains used St Margaret's Spur to connect to the high-level station and ran through to Tunbridge Wells West. Lingfield station, seen here in May 1994, once hosted raceday specials for the nearby racecourse, but that is now a matter of railway history. Approaching the station in appalling weather is the annual Chipman's Class 20-hauled weedkilling train. *Author*

▲ A scene that could have been recorded in many Welsh valleys in recent decades but which has now all but disappeared, is the sight of deep coal mines. In the depths of Ebbw Vale was Marine Colliery, which in 1913 employed over 2,400 men. In 1927 there was a local tragedy when an underground explosion killed 52 miners. The pit was integrated with Six Bells Colliery in 1970, but by March 1989 the entire complex had closed forever. Against an awesome industrial backdrop No 37284 runs round its train of old vacuum-braked hoppers, on a bleak day in 1986. *Author*

▼ Although branch passenger trains of earlier generations on the Ebbw Vale branch in South Wales have already been featured it would be remiss if an example of a steel train from the freight-only years was not included. Train 6B75 is of particular interest because the steel coils that are on their way to BSC Ebbw Vale for tinplating are hauled by Class 37/7 No 37886. This is one of the class not only to be re-geared and fitted with an alternator in place of the usual generator but one that also carried ballast weighing over 17 tons for tractive effort purposes. The location is north of Aberbeeg, on 25 April 1989. *Author*

▲ The last deep coal mine in the whole of South Wales was Tower Colliery, which was purchased from the National Coal Board by the actual pit workers in 1994, after closure had been announced. They used their redundancy money and a bank loan to raise the £2 million price tag. The mine finally closed in January 2008, the main seams having been exhausted. It had been the largest employer in the Cynon Valley. The photographer was fortunate to capture this Class 37 north-west of Aberdare hauling empty vacuum-braked wagons bound for Tower Colliery in 1986. *Author*

▼ When photographed in April 1989, four branch lines radiated from Tondu, some of them dividing into two or more other branches. Back in 1966 the route to the left went to Maesteg, Cymmer Afan and Glyncorrwg, and to the right to Raglan siding, Blaengarw and Nantymoel, while behind the photographer there was a branch down to the main line at Bridgend and another freight-only line to Margam. Access to all of these routes from the station area was controlled by Tondu box. Arriving from Maesteg washery with more vintage vacuum-braked hoppers is Railfreight No 37698 *Coedbach*, with a number on the front for the short-sighted spotter, and correct coal sector decals on the bodysides. *Author*

▲ Far below the chimney pots of Golant in Cornwall a massive double-headed china clay train runs along the causeway across the hamlet's little harbour beside the River Fowey. The train is running down the branch from Lostwithiel to Fowey, which since 1965 has been freight only. The line now stops slightly short of Fowey at Carne Point, effectively Fowey Docks. The number of trains has reduced over the years but there are normally at least two round trips per day between the port and the clay drying plants on the Newquay and/or Drinnick Mill branch lines. Nos 37196 and 37222 are seen in October 1985 hauling vacuum-braked wooden-bodied clay hood wagons that were finally withdrawn in February 1988. *Author*

1990s AND PRIVATISATION

By THE DAWN OF THE 1990s the romantic image of a rural weed-covered single-track branch line, with a single-coach train running a handful of miles with fewer passengers on board than could be counted on one hand, and arriving at a fully signalled and fully staffed terminus station, was a memory from the distant past. The seemingly perpetual reviews of the railways, their operations and above all their finances had removed hundreds of lines and thousands of stations from the railway network. However, in the 1980s in particular, closures of the remaining branch and minor lines had slowed considerably and a new culture had arrived in the corridors of power and in the minds of the public, based on concerns about emissions, global warming and traffic congestion, with 'green' credentials becoming fashionable. In enthusiast circles there had been an acceptance that surviving branches had managed a great escape.

Even though in pure profit-and-loss terms such lines were still loss-making, for the foreseeable future subsidies or grants would continue to be made and, indeed, the survivors are still with us in the 21st century. Under the privatisation franchisee contracts train operating companies (TOCs) would continue to provide such services but with accruing deficits being underwritten by the Government. The entire subject of privatisation of our railways is easily politicised, but it must be said that although instigated by the Conservative Party and opposed by the Labour Party, once in power the Labour Party did not reverse the process, not because there had been a change of opinion, but probably on the grounds of cost in reimbursing shareholders and the likely confusion that would no doubt arise.

Much has been written about the privatisation of British Rail(ways) and although there were a handful of plus points the consensus of opinion is that the process has not worked, at least to the extent originally envisaged. The British Railways Board favoured a privatisation that 'sold' the entire BR company as a single entity, but eventually there would be some 25 TOCs and over 100 companies and sub-contractors running what had formally been a single BR business, albeit with a hierarchical and compartmentalised organisation. Under privatisation the operating of trains, the supply of locomotives and rolling stock and the provision of the railway infrastructure, including track and signalling, were all separated. It appeared to many of the bidding companies that there were potentially rich pickings to be had, and indeed there were, until a recession reared its ugly head and the possibility of incurring operational losses became very real. This resulted in more than one high-profile default as a major company could not make the contracted contribution to the Government's coffers.

The thinking behind privatisation was that the Government wanted to rid itself of the perpetual burden of trying to run the railways profitably, having to provide never-ending subsidies from the public purse, having to provide significant capital for equipment procurements, and no doubt having to continually deal with confrontations with intransigent trade unions that threatened industrial action immediately any change to the status quo was mooted, whether or not it saved public funds or was in the interest of passengers. In the 1980s, the Government had privatised a number of the old unwieldy nationalised industries, including telecommunications in 1984, gas in 1986, water in 1989, and electricity in 1990. Now it was to be the turn of the railways. A broad-brush outline of the complex privatisation proposals and the problems encountered along the way follows.

Privatisation had been lurking in the wings for some time. Railway-related activities such as railway engineering, catering and advertising had effectively been privatised or 'outsourced' while under BR. Under sectorisation some aspects of privatisation such as competitive tendering, outside customer investment in rail freight and bringing in private capital to BR in terms of the freight wagon fleet and freight terminals had occurred. There had also been attempts to privatise the Gatwick Express service and, surprisingly, the Slough to Windsor branch line, but negotiations fizzled out. These episodes were followed by an idea of contracting out the London Tilbury & Southend line and there was even an attempt to sell the Settle & Carlisle line by competitive tender. During the late 1980s the BRB, the Government and it would seem every transport academic, expressed a view as to what form privatisation should take. There was no consensus. Various reports were produced but following a 1989/90 recession privatisation was again on the back burner. By 1991 the subject re-emerged, with John Major as Prime Minister. The Secretary of State (Minister) for Transport, Malcolm Rifkind, wrote to the BRB Chairman Bob Reid giving the options of selling BR as a whole, selling by business sector, selling by region, and separating BR into track and operating companies. Regional Railways would continue to receive a subsidy but would be offered on franchise to the lowest bidder. Various reports were commissioned from consultants at huge cost but they were inconclusive offering only a number of options. Exchanges continued but a general election was looming and the Conservative Party included aspects of rail privatisation in their manifesto. The Labour Party expected to win and they had told BR that when elected they would instruct BR to cease all work on privatisation. To the surprise of many the Conservatives were re-elected and so privatisation was again on the cards.

In July 1992 a 'New Opportunities for Railways' report was published. The Treasury had stated that 'no option would be accepted which retained a perpetual subsidy' as they were no doubt worried about the bottomless pit that they had thrown cash down for decades. Also, it was stated that 'no single solution is appropriate to all BR businesses'. The plan was for an independent track authority (Railtrack) with separate operating companies. Privatisation was to be completed within the lifetime of the new Parliament – maximum five years. Economists were pessimistic about success pointing out that there would be considerable complexities in the transfer pricing and costing mechanisms required.

The privatisation was formalised in the 1993 Transport Act. At Bill stage there had been over 500 amendments and plenty of opposition. Within BR the organisational structure to facilitate privatisation came into effect on 1 April 1994. Railtrack took over ownership of all track, signalling and stations. They let out over 2,500 stations to the franchised train operators, retaining control of the largest termini. However, the negotiation of track access charges was protracted, being finally agreed in March 1994. With the Tories facing almost certain defeat in the 1997 election they hastily privatised Railtrack during 1996. Privatisation had truly begun. The first passenger franchises were introduced in February 1996 (the first two having been awarded but not implemented in 1995). All 25 rail franchises had been awarded by March 1997.

Various aspects of rail regulation were introduced and a Rail Regulator appointed to police all aspects of the privatisation process. The role also included overseeing access charges for the TOCs, the franchisees that would run on the national rail network. A Director of Passenger Rail Franchising was responsible for the franchising process in transferring operations to 25 TOCs. The TOCs mostly hired their rolling stock from Rolling Stock Leasing Companies (ROSCOs). There were three ROSCOs and all passenger coaches, locomotives, and multiple units were transferred to them. Although companies changed hands the three-company structure remained unchanged for the first decade of privatisation, although they were joined by various small, short-term leasing companies.

Freight locomotives and ex-BR wagons were owned either by the freight train operators or their customer companies. The six freight operating companies were Mainline, Load-Haul, Trans-Rail, Railfreight Distribution, Freightliner, and Rail Express Systems. On 24 February 1996 the first three of these sectors were sold to North & South Railways, a subsidiary of the American company Wisconsin Central

Railroad, the British operation later being called English Welsh & Scottish Railways. They later acquired Railfreight Distribution in November 1996 and later still, Rail Express Systems. Subsequently, open-access freight operators such as Direct Rail Services and First Group GBRf joined the ranks of freight operators and, of course, all of these organisations worked trains over the branch and minor lines that we are primarily concerned with here.

Unfortunately for Railtrack, a number of serious railway accidents, allegedly caused by poor track and point maintenance, called into question their whole operation. There was suggestion that financial targets and budgets were affecting track replacement schedules, which ran the risk of compromising safety. Track and signal maintenance was taken back in house by Network Rail in 2004.

There have been many criticisms of privatisation since 1994 and although there have been a handful of recognised advantages in privatising the railways, overall there have been few performance indicators that have shown improvements over the last years of British Rail operation. It is difficult to logically order observations and so the following is something of a ragbag of comments. One of the main criticisms has been that the periods of franchise were not long enough for the companies to make long-term investments. Since the mid- to late 1990s franchisees have come and gone and there have been name and livery changes aplenty. At times it has been difficult for even students of the railways to keep up with never-ending change. There is no doubt that the ROSCOs were huge beneficiaries of the privatisation process and subsequent sales of both businesses and assets cost the exchequer some £900 million, generally regarded as a national scandal, with the Commons Public Accounts Committee offering scathing criticism of the Department of Transport.

One of the easiest ways of reducing costs is to reduce manpower, but several TOCs gave so many drivers voluntary redundancy deals that they left no contingency, leading to staff shortages and train cancellations. Certain unregulated fares were increased well above the rate of inflation. The ability to simply 'hop-on' an intercity train virtually disappeared as seat booking became mandatory on certain limited-capacity long-distance trains. The ROSCOs were again winners, charging large sums for TOCs to hire old stock that had already been 'written-off' in accounting terms on their balance sheets. After 15 years of privatisation statistics showed that the average age of all rolling stock was no less than it had been in BR days, although the situation has improved very recently.

For UK rolling stock manufacturers, privatisation has been a commercial disaster with large procurements from abroad and unbridgeable gaps in ordering schedules, leaving an almost skeleton UK manufacturing capability. Trains have been no more punctual than in the days of BR, despite the introduction of 'fiddles' where trains have scandalously been terminated part-way through

▲ Some would justifiably argue that the still-open GWR route from Castle Cary to Weymouth is neither a branch nor a minor railway, but it is single track for much of the distance and it is certainly not a major railway artery. Whatever the category, it provides an excuse for including a photograph of the truly delightful Yeovil Pen Mill station in Somerset, which is still controlled by semaphore signals. Using the double-faced platform road, 'Sprinter' No 150277 heads for Dorset in August 1993. This location and Maiden Newton are the only crossing points between Castle Cary and Dorchester West. *Author*

▶ Newquay in Cornwall still plays host to long-distance through trains in the peak summer months. The trains are filled with holidaymakers travelling to the Atlantic Coast resort from London, the north of England and Scotland. Although once a common practice, since 1979 this has been the only Cornish branch line and Newquay the only Cornish resort to benefit from through main line trains. Passing the spartan site of St Columb Road station in September 1993 is the Saturday IC125 working from London Paddington. There was a corresponding train in the opposite direction. In common with so many locations, the station once had permanent buildings, a passing loop, goods yard, signalbox and station staff. *Author*

▲ It seems hard to believe that even a 78-ton locomotive could safely travel over track embedded in visibly crumbling concrete but for a loaded boat train to be traversing the branch to Southampton Western Docks, even at slow speed, looks precarious. In September 1991 No 33101 draws its Network SouthEast Mark 2a coaches towards the terminal. The track mileage in the docks area is now but a fraction of what it once was due to containerisation, the loss of wagonload freight and the absence of the great Atlantic liners, although cruise ship traffic is on the increase. *Author*

▼ Yet another branch line obituary was written in 1995 when 154 years of railway history ended as the last MoD train left Bedenham, between Fareham and Gosport in Hampshire. The first train operated to Gosport in November 1841 and it was to become famous for its associations with Queen Victoria and her visits to the Isle of Wight. Lines ran beyond Gosport to Clarence Yard and also to Stokes Bay, with another branch between Fort Brockhurst to Lee-on-the-Solent. Passenger services ceased back in 1953, ticket income having suffered from bus competition. Goods services at Gosport ceased in January 1969 leaving just the irregular military traffic at Bedenham. In May 1991, No 47354 heads munitions wagons towards Fareham. The line was to become part of a tramway system but rising costs resulted in the scheme being put on the back burner, for now. *Author*

their journey to avoid lateness on the back working, with passengers being unceremoniously dumped on a platform to wait for the next train. The author has experienced this appalling situation with the 'Southern' TOC. Another disgraceful practice is to build in ridiculous amounts of recovery time, just to ensure an 'on-time' or only slightly late arrival. For example, on First Great Western London to Penzance 'High Speed' services up to 18 minutes are allowed for the 5.75-mile journey from St Erth to Penzance, an average speed of 19mph, whereas an up local stopping train takes eight minutes! In 1902, the equivalent down journey time from St Erth to Penzance was ten minutes. Taking the most charitable view, that is a full eight minutes of recovery time, presumably to avoid financial penalties for lateness.

The upgrading of the West Coast Main Line was intended to deliver a 140mph railway at a cost of £2 billion, whereas what was actually delivered was a 125mph railway at a cost of £9 billion. As regards branch and minor lines it was always recognised that while the Government required TOCs to run and maintain unprofitable but socially desirable services there would be a need for public subsidy, because

no business-orientated commercial undertaking would consider for one moment running an unremunerative service. However, it was hoped that under privatisation there would be an injection of private capital and while that has happened to some degree the amounts involved have been inadequate to prevent Government subsidies from spiralling.

In 1994, Government support for BR was a massive £1,627 million but within a decade support from all sources totalled an unbelievable £4,593 million, in current price terms, well over twice as much as with the nationalised undertaking. A negative aspect for profitability has been a significant rise in wages in real terms since 1994. In spite of privatisation, Government interference in the railways is as strong as ever, although problems with Railtrack and certain franchisee failures have required an element of intervention. Overall, and in the context of subsidy, privatisation would seem to have been an abject failure, but that has not been reflected in the number of passengers travelling by rail, at least until the 2008–10 recession, which until then had increased by 40 per cent compared with BR days. In view of this mixed assessment the privatisation jury

▶ For several decades there was a shuttle service between Clapham Junction and Kensington Olympia. For many years the service ran only in the morning and evening rush hours, used mainly by the staff of a large Post Office installation at 'Kenny O'. Olympia was, and still is, an interesting place to observe cross-London freight traffic and it is also the terminus of an LT Underground branch from Earls Court. The site was a Motorail terminal for a number of years and inter-regional services also stopped at the station. The line was electrified and services were extended to Willesden and more recently, Watford Junction. In this view, NSE route-learning ex-Class 416/2 EMU No 931001 stands beside a District Line tube train. *Author*

◄ Another photograph of the interesting and diverse Seaford branch line, but on this occasion showing the rare phenomenon of a diesel-hauled train at the platform. In April 1990, Hunslet-Barclay Class 20 No 20901 is ready to return to Lewes with a weedkilling train, while 4-CIG Class 424/1 No 1717 arrives from Brighton at the now-lifted bay platform. The signalbox in the background closed in 1977 and that too has since been demolished. Control of the line is undertaken from Newhaven. *Author*

is, perhaps, still out but the smart money is probably on failure, due to the continuing vast subsidies.

In terms of branch and minor lines there have been important developments in the creation of Community Rail, supported by Network Rail. Community Rail schemes are intended to involve the local community in the running, development and costs of rural rail routes with the objective of providing a long-term future for such lines. Network Rail is trying to embrace a range of local individuals and organisations ranging from user groups to the friends of certain stations, by forming Community Rail partnerships all over the UK. At the time of writing Community Rail routes include the Abbey Line from Watford to St Albans Abbey, the Penistone Line from Huddersfield to Barnsley, the Barton Line from Barton-upon-Humber to Cleethorpes, the Bittern Line from North Walsham to Sheringham, the Derwent Valley Line from Matlock to Derby, the East Lancashire Line from Preston to Colne, the Esk Valley Line from Middlesbrough to Whitby, the Gainsborough Line from Sudbury to Marks Tey, the Island Line from Ryde Pier to Shanklin, the Lakes Line from Oxenholme to Windermere, the Looe Valley Line from Liskeard to Looe, the Lymington to Brockenhurst line, the Maritime Line from Falmouth to Truro, the St Ives Bay Line from St Erth to St Ives, the South Fylde Line from Preston to Blackpool South, the Tamar Valley Line from Plymouth (St Budeaux) to Gunnislake, the Tarka Line from Exeter (Cowley Bridge) to Barnstaple, the Atlantic Coast Line from Par to Newquay, the Clitheroe Line from Manchester to Clitheroe, the Marston Line from Bedford to Bletchley, the Medway Line from Strood to Paddock Wood, the Poacher Line from Grantham to Skegness, the Severn Beach Line from Bristol (Narroways Hill Junction) to Severn Beach, the Wherry Line from Norwich to Lowestoft and Great Yarmouth, the North Staffordshire Line from Crewe to Stoke-on-Trent and Derby, and the Cumbrian Line from Carlisle to Barrow-in-Furness. It is hoped that all of these lines will have a secure future and the list clearly demonstrates that despite the post-Beeching closures this is still very much a branch line Britain.

Finally, there has been much talk about the reopening of long-closed branch and minor lines, which have the potential of giving greater access to the railway system for some 1.75 million people. Pro-rail organisations ranging from Campaign for Better Transport (formerly Transport 2000) and specific User Groups, to Railfuture and Transport Britain have produced lists of lines that in the view of some of these organisations could usefully be reopened. One lists 136 routes which, in their view, should be reopened, although catering for the crowds at Trawsfynydd who want to travel to Blaenau Ffestiniog might not be taken too seriously by those writing the cheques! The movement gained a little more credibility when, in 2009, the then current TOCs publicly stated that they had identified 14 lines, which could become viable financially. However, it was noticeable that while they gave this prospect their 'unprecedented backing' they were not offering to pay for the reopenings!

While every railfan and probably every reader of this book would dearly love to see some of these closed lines reopened, the prospect of the exchequer parting with a conservative estimate of half a billion pounds in the middle of a recession and with the UK deeply in debt is little more than whistling in the wind. If there was money to be made in reopening some of these previously little-used lines then there would be a queue of entrepreneurs waiting at the door – and there are not. Some lines have reopened, for example to Ebbw Vale and Alloa, but with pressure on Council Tax rates and with taxation being increased to refill the Treasury's depleted coffers we are probably lucky to have retained as many branches and minor lines as we have. We must reflect not only on all that we have lost, as shown in the illustrations within this book, but perhaps be thankful that subsidies are still continuing to underwrite the cost of running the branches which have, miraculously, survived perpetual reviews.

▶ For the branch and minor line fan a season spent with the annual weedkilling train would be utterly fascinating as almost every line on the national network is treated with chemicals. Photographically, the trains were welcome because they broadly ran to a timetable, which was a significantly better proposition than waiting for a non-existent 'Q' path train, an 'as-and-when-required' goods that was not required, or a freight train running 280 minutes late! Normally, it was a tough proposition getting a shot of a train at Cattewater Junction, Plymouth, but in April 1990 Nos 20901 and 20904 duly obliged, as they traversed the freight-only line. On the right is the line to Plymstock that closed in February 1989. *Author*

▶ The first station out of Exeter on the Barnstaple branch is Newton St Cyres. The track is now single with only two passing places between Cowley Bridge Junction and Barnstaple, although this may be increased. Few trains stop at the station and then only by request. The 39-mile branch is now marketed as the 'Tarka Line' and a number of improvements have recently been made. However, privatisation has not cured all the problems and often, when only a single or two-car diesel unit is employed, trains are hopelessly overcrowded. In February 1993, Regional Railways Class 153 'Sprinter' No 153380 speeds by on its way to Exeter St David's. Most trains work to and from Exmouth. *Author*

▶ This slightly unusual view illustrates the single-track Gunnislake branch, but at a location that was once the double-track SR main line from Exeter to Plymouth. Running beside the River Tamar and approaching the Royal Albert Bridge is Regional Railways 'Sprinter' No 150241 with an up working in April 1993. The train will have reversed direction at Bere Alston. The river separates the counties of Devon and Cornwall and the train will have visited both during its journey. It is easy to see why the line is marketed as the 'Tamar Valley Line'. *Author*

◀ Exeter Central was the primary Exeter station for the LSWR/SR, not only in terms of their main line from London Waterloo but in respect of connections to a plethora of branch lines in north Devon and north Cornwall. This network was known as the 'withered arm' after the closures of the 1960s. The station was far better placed for the city centre than the GWR St David's station, but from the early 1960s it became a poor second place to its former rival in terms of train services. A branch train from Exmouth to Newton Abbot is seen arriving at Exeter Central station. *Author*

◀ On some of the more geographically remote branch lines it was good to have information about any special workings. In the days before the internet and mobile telephones it was often a combination of special traffic notices and cooperative railway staff that produced the required 'gen'. Based on such information an inspection saloon was photographed working over the Pembroke Dock branch on 2 August 1983 and is seen south of Narbeth behind No 37302. Without information one could wait 12 months for another! *Author*

▼ It is easy to become emotional when observing the conversion to offices of a rather grand, listed 135-year-old station building to make way for a large, modern traincare depot in readiness for Class 159 operations between Waterloo and Exeter. The original GWR branch line terminus at Salisbury was hidden away to the north of the current station. It had not seen a passenger train since 1932 when services were diverted to the LSWR/SR station. As a broad-gauge extension from the GWR's Warminster branch the line reached Salisbury in Wiltshire during 1856 (three years ahead of the LSWR's arrival in the city), and was converted to standard gauge in 1874. The tracks in this view were about to be lifted, demonstrating the value of photography in recording the ever-evolving railway scene. *Author*

► There is nothing more depressing than arriving at your annual holiday destination in pouring rain, but that is precisely what this passenger would experience on arrival at St Ives in Cornwall on this day in August 1992. With the train guard providing portering duties the train has the road at St Erth station, the first stop being the 'park-and-ride' station of Lelant Saltings. In 1877, the St Ives branch was the last in Cornwall to be built to broad-gauge specification and, following a change of gauge in 1892, it is still going strong. *Author*

▼ This study depicts the traditional role of the junction station as passengers alight from the Stourbridge Town branch train at Stourbridge Junction and make their way across the adjacent platform for their main line connection, mostly for Birmingham New Street. Nine passengers, half of them youngsters, make that transfer while another group board single power car No M55012 for the ¾-mile return journey (see page 129). *Author*

▲ This branch train is using a small segment of the former through route between Oxford and Cambridge. The cross-country line is open to passenger traffic between Oxford and Bicester Town station and from Bletchley to Bedford but this section from Bicester to Bletchley has been freight-only since the beginning of 1968. In May 1992, original Railfreight-liveried No 31234 is seen at Steeple Claydon with an Akeman Street to Ince & Elton train of empty UK Fertiliser wagons plus a brakevan. Consultants have produced a costed feasibility report for the East West Rail Consortium that could see passenger trains running on these metals by 2017. *Author*

▼ South of the previous location on the old Metropolitan & Great Central Railway Joint Line is Quainton Road station, until December 1935 the junction for the Oxford & Aylesbury Tramroad branch to Brill. The Buckinghamshire Railway Centre has now occupied the site for many years and preservationists have restored the station. Occasionally, NSE in the past and now Chiltern Trains, run units to the old station for open days and special occasions. Otherwise, it is mainly 'Binliner' waste trains to Calvert that use the freight-only line. A Class 165 turbo diesel unit is seen at the station in April 1992. *Author*

▲ For several decades the Bedford to Bletchley branch was something of a time warp with old DMUs rattling past manual crossing gates, semaphore signals, open-air crossing keeper ground frames, low platforms with wooden step access, and oil lamps. Gradually, modernisation crept its way along the line, including these crossing barriers at Woburn Sands station. Green-liveried No W55023 slows for the station on its way to Bletchley in August 1993. The advert on the right is best ignored! *Author*

▼ The surface of the very low platform at Millbrook station is covered in local bricks, but in certain lighting conditions they resemble cobbles. Other than for athletes capable of leaping on to the branch train, these wooden steps were provided for easier access. This practice survived well into the 1990s. The green-liveried single power car was a welcome visitor to the line so late in its career, giving the impression that the photograph had been taken 25 years earlier. No W55023, alias unit No L123, is heading for Bletchley in August 1993. Note the semaphore signal in the background. *Author*

▲ High conifers have obscured much of the old 1873-built railway site at Marlow, which by November 1991 had been reduced to a single-line stub from Bourne End, where trains reverse before continuing on their 7¼-mile journey to Maidenhead. At Bourne End the line from Maidenhead once continued through to High Wycombe, but that section was closed in 1970. A NSE-liveried two-car Class 101 DMU, No L207, forms a mid-afternoon departure and it is hoped that the husband, wife and three children have a family railcard. *Author*

▼ Compared with earlier photographs within these pages this November 1991 view shows BR had demolished the fine old Henley-on-Thames terminus building, completed platform and awning modifications, undertaken considerable filling-in, and tidied the now somewhat clinical site. Maintenance costs will be minimal, making a very small dent in BR's balance sheet. About to depart for Twyford and Reading is two-car DMU No L202, which will also stop at the intermediate stations of Shiplake and Wargrave. *Author*

▲ Chappel & Wakes Colne is an intermediate station on the Marks Tey to Sudbury branch, which was once part of a much longer through route. Chappel is now the home of the East Anglian Railway Museum. It was also the point where the Colne Valley & Halstead Railway diverged towards Haverhill, until services over that line were withdrawn at the end of 1961. In September 1993, Class 156 No 156413 is seen arriving from Sudbury. The signals, the old coach body and the sidings are located on museum property. *Author*

▼ There are mile upon mile of railway lines in the Metropolis that are elevated and rest on brick railway arches, a product of the Victorian age. Many of the apertures are occupied by business and storage premises, albeit offering something of a 'back street' appearance. When photographed on 18 February 1994, the 12¼-mile Barking to Gospel Oak service was one of the last bastions of the diesel-mechanical unit and, here, No L721 is seen approaching Leytonstone High Road with a Gospel Oak service. The roadside litter is a sad reflection on modern UK society, the 1983 Litter Act seemingly being an unenforceable irrelevance. *Author*

▲ It would be logical to expect a main line train to be given preference over a minor or branch train. Indeed, the two normally run in different priority train identity headcode categories. However, in this April 1992 view the single-car Class 153 unit coming off the Central Wales line at Craven Arms has clearly been given preference over the Class 158 Cardiff to Manchester service on the main line, visible in the distance. No 153312 has already been on the move for over three hours from its Swansea starting point. There are just four trains per day in each direction over the line, a surprising survivor. *Author*

▼ This delightful setting is at Bargoed on the Cardiff to Rhymney branch line. Most services on the line run from Rhymney to either Penarth or Barry Island but some start and terminate at the intermediate station of Bargoed. In this interesting movement from March 1993, a four-coach train from Penarth and Cardiff Central, comprising Class 150 and Class 143 units leaves the platform for Rhymney, while in the background a Class 150, which is a Bargoed starter, waits to enter the platform to collect at least ten passengers. *Author*

▲ Increasingly over the years, branch line termini have been reduced to single-line stubs with trains operating from a single platform. This has also happened at Rhymney, witness the abandoned island platform, however; a number of overnight berthing sidings have been retained, as seen here in March 1993. Of the two units awaiting departure the Class 150 will offer the better ride for passengers, but the Class 143 four-wheeler will offer better visibility. Cardiff is only 23¼ miles away, but the journey time is almost an hour. *Author*

▼ Little and large at Blaenau Ffestiniog. The 133-ton monster on the left is a BR standard gauge English Electric Class 40, No 40131, which was working an 'Adex' special to the town of slate, whereas on the right is a Ffestiniog Railway, 1ft 11½in-gauge, 24-ton Fairlie steam locomotive that is leaving for Portmadoc. The 28-mile branch from Llandudno Junction is still very much in business, although services are sometimes disrupted by a flooded River Conwy (see page 143). *Author*

▲ Single-line tokens came in all shapes and sizes, from small alloy 'keys' to long wooden 'staffs' with engraved brass nameplates. There were a variety of signalling systems employed on the branches with some tokens being exchanged with signalmen while others were placed in pouches and surrendered via crude catching equipment. In some cases, simple token possession was paramount, while in other areas tokens needed to be inserted into Electric Token Instruments before line possession could be given. Whatever the system, safety was of course uppermost. The token for the Chatham Dockyard branch is seen here. *Author*

◄ A Ministry of Defence policeman exchanges greetings with the second man on board Railfreight-liveried Class 33 'Crompton' No 33042 in February 1992 as it descends from Gillingham to Chatham Dockyard. Chatham was once a huge naval dockyard dating back to 1567, in the days of HM Queen Elizabeth I. It closed in 1984 but residues of contaminated soil were discovered and some years were spent removing the substance by rail. It was conveyed in sealed containers for disposal at the old brickworks siding at Forders in Bedfordshire, near Stewartby on the Bedford to Bletchley branch. Note the magnificent London Chatham & Dover Railway lower quadrant signal, with low-aspect glasses. *Author*

▶ If any reader was an enthusiast of English Electric DEMUs they could have done no better than staying overnight in the Windmill Guest House at Rye in East Sussex, seen here on the right. Crossing the River Tillingham is a Network South East three-car unit making its way from Hastings to Ashford. It always seemed curious, that following electrification of the Tonbridge to Hastings and Kent Coast lines, the link between the two was never similarly converted, especially after closure notices were withdrawn, ensuring a long-term future for the line. Class 170s now work the route. There was once a nearby branch to Rye Harbour and also the narrow-gauge Camber Tramway, but both have long since closed. *Author*

▼ The only train that normally works across the Romney Marshes on part of the old branch line to New Romney is the nuclear flask traffic to and from the power station at Dungeness. However, on 13 November 1993 an engineers' train appeared at Lydd Town hauled by No 33063. The train had left Hoo Junction at 06.00 and having dropped ballast further down the branch it is seen here returning to Hoo as train 6Z17. The old station has been disused since passenger services ceased in March 1967. *Brian Morrison*

▲ The Merehead branch in Somerset comprises the south-eastern section of the old GWR Witham to Yatton line. Over the years, millions of tons of stone and aggregates removed from the surrounding hills have made their way along the branch to an immense number of locations, largely in the south-east of England. In the mid-1980s, ageing British-built diesel power was replaced by sophisticated and technologically advanced North American diesel locomotives, hugely increasing both trainload weight and motive power reliability. Eventually, 'jumbo trains' with a gross weight of about 4,000 tons operated out of Merehead to Westbury and beyond. In May 1991, at the eastern end of Merehead Quarry Loop Junction, a Foster Yeoman Class 59 heads air-braked 50-tonne hoppers away from the complex. *Author*

▼ Another stone and aggregate freight-only branch line runs from Crediton to Meldon Quarry, beyond Okehampton. The quarry once supplied most of the Southern Region's ballast requirements, but in recent years operations have been something of a 'stop/start' process. However, in February 1993 business was booming as Dutch-liveried 'Cromptons' Nos 33103 and 33057 *Seagull* arrived from Tonbridge in Kent with a load of empty 'Seacow' ballast hoppers. The site is presently the home of the Dartmoor Railway, now owned by Iowa Pacific Holdings, trading as the Devon & Cornwall Railway, and who have applied to Network Rail for access to Exeter for both passenger and freight services. The line was of course once part of the LSWR main line between Exeter and Plymouth. *Author*

▲ The necessary telephoto lens gives the impression that there has been a massive derailment of bogie tank wagons at Quidhampton, near Salisbury. Following the abandonment of the old GWR/Western Region route into the city, when the track configuration at Wilton Junction was rationalised, this section remained in use for calcium carbonate trains from the adjacent English China Clay works. These changes effectively created a short, freight-only branch line. In May 1991, No 47112 was the train engine, with the works located through the cutting on the right and the Wilton Junction access line on the left. *Author*

▼ During the last couple of decades of BR's existence far more branches to industrial installations and freight terminals were closed, compared with passenger-carrying lines. This was especially the case in the coal mining areas of Nottinghamshire and Derbyshire where the railway map was transformed as the coal industry dwindled and pits closed on an almost weekly basis. In this spectacular view at Bolsover Coalite works, No 58031, an example of BR's penultimate freight locomotive offering, shunts HEA coal wagons on 23 July 1994. The works is now closed, the buildings razed and the track lifted. Passenger trains last passed near to this spot in July 1930! *Gavin Morrison*

▲ When the Merseyside Class 503 electrics were withdrawn in 1984/85 they were replaced by Class 508 units, which had mostly been transferred from the Southern Region. Several aspects of their design were based on the prototype 4-PEP sliding-door unit. Overlooked by the surviving signalbox and associated signals at the Wirral terminus of West Kirby on 9 August 1990, Merseyrail No 508134 heads for the platform and the waiting crowds, while No 508104 is berthed in adjacent sidings. *Gavin Morrison*

▼ Another Class 508 EMU, No 508118, is seen here at New Brighton, another terminus at the end of a short branch from Bidston Junction on the Wirral side of the River Mersey, a few miles north of Birkenhead. Somewhat surprisingly the town enjoys a 15-minute interval train service throughout much of the day, until mid-evening when it becomes half-hourly. All trains work through to Liverpool Central and Liverpool Lime Street. The scene was recorded on 12 January 1995. *Gavin Morrison*

▲ The line from Blackburn to Clitheroe and Hellifield remains open but has had a mixed history in passenger train terms. Passenger services along the old Victorian Lancashire & Yorkshire Railway route via Clitheroe became a victim of the 1960s, closing in September 1962. It remained open for freight and diversions away from the West Coast Main Line that were routed over the Settle & Carlisle line. However, pressure to reopen what is now called the 'Ribble Valley Line' saw passenger services reinstated as far as Clitheroe in 1994. No 150214 departs from a restored Clitheroe station on 6 January 1995, Manchester Victoria being the usual destination. *Gavin Morrison*

▼ Milngavie is at the end of an old North British branch (originally the Glasgow & Milngavie Junction Railway), about 8½ rail miles north of Glasgow. It enjoys a frequent service to both Glasgow Central and Queen Street. The branch was electrified in 1959 and subsequently the tail end of the line was singled. A third platform was removed at the terminus in 1983. Here, Strathclyde-liveried EMU No 303058 stands at one of two remaining platform roads on 10 June 1992, apparently 'Not in service'! *Gavin Morrison*

▲ Study of a pre-Grouping railway gazetteer shows a myriad of lines in the environs of Thornton Junction in Fife. A minor line connected Thornton Junction with Leuchars Junction via a coastal route than ran via Leven, Crail and St Andrews. The line closed to passengers in stages between 1965 and 1969 with just a rump to Methil at the Thornton end of the line surviving for freight use. With the large Scottish Grain Distillers works in the background a Pathfinder Chartex is a rare visitor to the line, seen passing Cameron Bridge on 15 August 1992 behind Mainline-liveried No 37152. The wide island platform is disused. *Gavin Morrison*

▼ Long after closure to passengers of the Alva to Cambus branch line, east of Stirling, in November 1954, the line remained open for goods traffic. However, these services were cut back from Alva to Menstrie and Glenochil in February 1964. Distilleries at Cambus and Menstrie, including the Glenochil yeast plant that handled tank wagons of molasses, continued to be served until 1993, when all traffic ceased. On 12 June 1991, Class 26 No 26041 in large logo original Railfreight livery leaves Menstrie with molasses tanks. A last visit for passengers occurred in 1992 when a DMU Chartex worked the branch. *Gavin Morrison*

▲ The railway line through Chirk and Ruabon is not really a minor line, but since the withdrawal of GWR/WR long-distance express trains, the closure of the Mid-Wales line, a reduction in steel traffic, the collapse of Wrexham & Shropshire Railway services and the singling of the line between Wrexham and Chester, it has become less important than it once was. A Chester to Shrewsbury DMU crosses the impressive Cefn Viaduct in April 1991. The fine, 17-arch structure spanning the River Dee, is 147ft high and 1,508ft long. *Author*

▼ Truly the end of the Wensleydale branch are these stop blocks at Redmire. Prior to the 1950s passengers could travel through from Northallerton to Garsdale via Hawes, but the line closed in two stages, during 1954 and 1959 respectively. In comparatively recent times a freight worked up the branch to a Tarmac Company quarry, but that traffic ended during the week the photograph was taken. On 15 December 1992, Class 60 No 60023 positions its wagons under the loading mechanism (top left). *Gavin Morrison*

▲ By the 1990s the freight-by-rail organisation on BR was changing rapidly following the business-orientated sectorisation processes of the 1980s. In 1994, Trainload Freight's sector was relaunched with three divisions: Transrail, LoadHaul and Mainline, effectively shadow freight companies. The bulk of operations within these divisions was purchased in 1996 by Wisconsin Central Railroad (trading as English, Welsh & Scottish Railways (EWS)). Class 37 No. 37670 will soon be in EWS ownership as it descends from the Luxulyan Valley at the southern end of the Newquay branch and approaches St Blazey Gate with a rake of loaded CDA china clay wagons from the ECC Rocks works at Goonbarrow Junction to Carne Point, Fowey. The River Par races by as, top right, the old engine house of Fowey Consuls mine stands as a silent sentinel from the 19th century. *Author*

DIESEL AND ELECTRIC CONSOLIDATION

▲ The last years of BR's existence and the start of privatisation saw branch and minor line consolidation. Indeed, a number of lines and stations were both opened and in some cases reopened, adding to the railway map for the first time in many years. Some of the reopenings were a direct result of Passenger Transport Executive PTE) involvement and local subsidy. This chapter shows the 'handover' years and the first years of privatisation of the former BR network. This was the scene at the Bishop Auckland terminus in June 2005 as four-wheeler No 142071 waited to leave for Saltburn. In times past Bishop Auckland was a grand station and the hub of five different North Eastern Railway rail routes, but is now merely a single-line stub. *Author*

▼ The delightful North Eastern Railway station building at Saltburn survives but not for its original purpose. In the summer months the current station platform is gaily decorated with flowers and hanging baskets, as seen on the right. In this scene the train guard having just provided a loading ramp to assist a disabled passenger adjusts his tie and collar on a warm summer's day. No 142071 has arrived from Bishop Auckland (see above) and will now return to Darlington. These much-criticised units do have the advantage of good visibility, even if travel sometimes resembles a fairground ride. *Author*

▲ The lovely old town of Whitby is still rail served by Esk Valley services from Middlesbrough. The coastal Middlesbrough to Scarborough route is long gone and there has been significant rationalisation in the station area, but the line is a great survivor. In recent years trains have worked through on Network Rail metals from the North Yorkshire Moors Railway. In June 2003, a three-car Class 144 unit No 144021 has just arrived and will soon be returning to Middlesbrough, 35 miles away by rail. *Author*

▼ Harrogate was once a hub of a quite sizeable North Eastern Railway wheel, with six quite different lines converging on the town. Over the years many have closed with perhaps the main route north (from Leeds) to Northallerton via Ripon being the most significant. By March 1967 only a passenger line from Leeds via Headingly to York survived, which was mostly worked as two separate lines that happened to meet in Harrogate. The line from Leeds to Harrogate has supported through IC125 trains to London, but from Harrogate to York, much of the route has been singled and could now reasonably be called a branch. In July 1996, Class 141 four-wheeler No 55541 has just arrived from York, with typical Yorkshire stone buildings in the background. The colourful livery is still embellished with tiny versions of the BR double arrows. *Author*

▲ One of the attractions of travelling the branches has always been spotting the curious or unusual, whether it be the trains themselves or some artefact or piece of railway paraphernalia. One is accustomed to finding railway mileposts on the ground, but this example at Ilkley is high up in the station awning. It shows that the station is 211¼ miles from London. *Author*

▼ A pleasant if not particularly scenic branch is the old Great Central Railway line to Barton-upon-Humber. The current train service frequency is two-hourly with a few extras. Most trains work to and from Cleethorpes. At Barton there are bus connections for Hull, which is accessed via the River Humber road suspension bridge. A bus service replaced the ferry crossing from New Holland Pier, immediately the new road crossing was ready for service in 1981. No 153319 is seen at the buffer stops in June 2005. *Author*

▲ The original granite terminus building at St Ives in Cornwall was sacrificed for the motor car in 1971 when the basic concrete replacement seen here was built further from the town. The branch has benefited from a 'park-and-ride' scheme where motorists leave their cars at Lelant Saltings and let the train take the strain. Wessex Trains' pictogram livery on vinyl has been applied to unit No 150241, which will shortly be departing for St Erth, in September 2006. The line is now operated by First Great Western. *Author*

▼ Almost a decade after the operational end of British Rail and under the auspices of First Great Western, Network Rail and the Devon and Cornwall Rail Partnership, the 'old days' were recalled when chocolate and cream station signs, including totems, were incorporated in a 2008 Liskeard station refurbishment. This shows the Looe branch platform, which is set at right angles to the main line station. In this September 2008 shot, No 153382 will soon be on its way down to Coombe Junction where it will reverse for the journey to Looe. *Author*

► A subsidised branch passenger service that has run for several years on peak season summer Sundays is from Exeter Central to Okehampton. The former LSWR/SR main line between Exeter and Plymouth had closed between Okehampton and Bere Alston in 1968, but in 1972 the remaining Crediton to Okehampton branch also closed, leaving only BR traffic to Meldon Quarry (however, see page 194). In September 2000, No 158841 prepares to return to Exeter, the wet weather no doubt reducing the number of travellers on this day. *Author*

► It is good to report that in a handful of examples there have been positive branch and minor line developments in the post-BR era. During 2009, a passing loop arrangement was installed at Penryn on the Falmouth branch, which last had such facilities back in the 1970s. This enabled the operation of a half-hourly service, the most frequent in the near 150-year history of the line. In 2005, before the introduction of the new service, No 153382, in 'Scenic Lines Devon and Cornwall' black and gold livery, pauses at Perranwell station on the down run. *Author*

► Just about the only item of infrastructure to survive the passage of time at Falmouth Docks has been this long awning with a curved corrugated-iron roof. The fine original station, signalbox, engine shed, turntable, sidings, goods shed and active docks connection have all gone, leaving a very spartan scene. On a fine day in October 1994, a Network SouthEast transferee, DMU No L723, waits for time before departure for Truro. New-generation replacement units were not far away. *Author*

▲ One of the better examples of a fully operational station on a weed-infested line that was still open to passengers was at Mitcham on the Wimbledon to West Croydon route. Arriving on the singled track in May 1997 is one of the ugly Class 456 two-car EMUs. Note the depressing state of the platform with every wall, cabinet and lamp post covered in graffiti by feeble-minded adolescents. This line was temporarily closed in 1997 and became part of the Croydon Tramlink system, so perhaps there was no point in spending scarce funds on maintenance of the 'run-down' infrastructure at that time. *Author*

▼ Another candidate in the weed-covered line competition would be this May 1997 view of Woodside on the doomed Elmers End to Addiscombe branch. Two-car Class 466 'Networker' No 466007 pauses on the down run. This line also closed in 1997 partly to become a section of the new Croydon Tramlink (now London Tramlink). It is hard to believe that the photographer was a passenger on the train and an obliging train crew waited for him to run down the platform, climb and descend the stairs via the old elevated station in the background, on to the old up platform, take the picture, negotiate the platform and stairs again to rejoin the train, an Olympian feat! *Author*

▲ This totally rural landscape features Birchden Junction, near the Sussex/Kent border, where the line from Tunbridge Wells West and Groombridge joined the Oxted to Uckfield line. Just days before the former route closed to passengers in July 1985, a Network SouthEast 3H DEMU is seen thumping past the signalbox. Spa Valley Railway trains now pass this spot since their extension plans to reach Eridge finally came to fruition. Southern is now the post-BR train operator on the surviving Uckfield line. *Author*

▼ It is difficult to keep up to date with the ever-changing Train Operating Company (TOC) franchises. However, after BR(SR) days, the NSE sector became the operator of the Uckfield branch and under privatisation this gave way to Connex, or Connex South Central to be precise. The TOC is now Southern, which is owned by Govia, a joint venture between the Go-Ahead and Keolis companies! How one longs for the end of such corporate complexities and the return of 'BR'! In June 2003, DEMU No 205205, painted in Connex yellow and white livery, will shortly be leaving Uckfield for London Victoria. For some time this unit operated with a trailer coach from a 4-CEP EMU coupled between the carriages seen here. In 2009/10 a new Uckfield station was built on this site, the original being located across the adjacent main road. *Author*

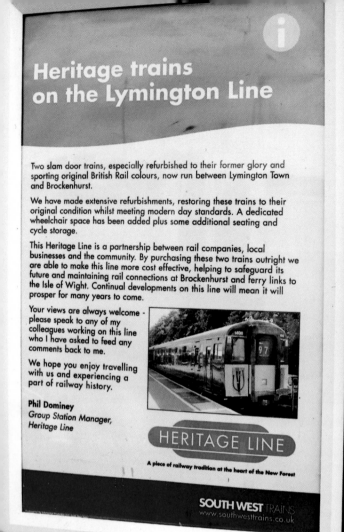

Heritage trains on the Lymington Line

Two slam door trains, especially refurbished to their former glory and sporting original British Rail colours, now run between Lymington Town and Brockenhurst.

We have made extensive refurbishments, restoring these trains to their original condition whilst meeting modern day standards. A dedicated wheelchair space has been added plus some additional seating and cycle storage.

This Heritage Line is a partnership between rail companies, local businesses and the community. By purchasing these two trains outright we are able to make this line more cost effective, helping to safeguard its future and maintaining rail connections at Brockenhurst and ferry links to the Isle of Wight. Continual developments on this line will mean it will prosper for many years to come.

Your views are always welcome - please speak to any of my colleagues working on this line who I have asked to feed any comments back to me.

We hope you enjoy travelling with us and experiencing a part of railway history.

Phil Dominey
Group Station Manager,
Heritage Line

HERITAGE LINE
A piece of railway tradition at the heart of the New Forest

SOUTH WEST TRAINS
www.southwesttrains.co.uk

◄ Although there have been innumerable problems in the overall privatisation process there have also been some chinks of light from the enthusiasts' perspective. During 2005, to the surprise of many, South West Trains identified the commercial potential of actively marketing the fact that they had decided to retain a couple of the otherwise extinct Class 421/7 'slam-door' three-car EMUs (modified with central locking doors) for use on the Brockenhurst to Lymington branch line. This poster appeared on local stations during 2006, with the BR totem being incorporated in the design. The old units soldiered on until May 2010. *Author*

▼ They seem to have been breeding bus shelters on the single-platform Lymington Pier station, a poor substitute for the earlier more traditional structure. In Stagecoach livery, this Class 421/5 'Greyhound' EMU, No 1316, arrives from Brockenhurst. At the pier, most passengers transfer to the Isle of Wight ferry for the short journey across the Solent to Yarmouth. As already mentioned, this was the last steam-hauled traditional branch on BR before the line was electrified in 1967. Curiously, when the vintage EMUs were withdrawn in May 2010 they were replaced on weekdays by diesel traction! *Author*

▲ When looking at the remains of the lovely old Gosport station over very many years the expression 'Rest in Peace' came to mind. Although the track, signals and most of the infrastructure had been ripped up after closure the main up side buildings and the superb colonnade were preserved, as seen here in 1994. The 1840s building was designed by Sir William Tite, who also designed the Royal Exchange in London. It was in the classic Italianate style with Tuscan columns and Corinthian capitals. The station has links with Queen Victoria who, in the early days passed here on her way to Clarence Pier when visiting the Isle of Wight. The temptation to interfere with this fitting memorial proved too much for the local authority and a scheme to incorporate housing and office buildings on the site was approved in 2006. It seems that nothing is sacred in this day and age. *Author*

▼ This picture spans generations and combines privatisation with the days of good old BR. The scene is Marchwood on the Fawley branch in Hampshire in March 2003. By then the old BR branch had been closed to passengers for 37 years but remained open for freight. Semaphore signals survived and in the background can be seen some manually controlled crossing gates by the erstwhile station. Traversing the line with a handful of oil tankers from Eastleigh is a shiny EWS Class 66, nicknamed 'Sheds'. No 66049 is about to leave the passing loop and enter another single-track section down to the refinery at Fawley. As already mentioned, the line is a candidate for reopening to passenger trains. *Author*

▲ It is a pleasure to have reason to be positive about something modern that thrives in the privatised railway world. For some time, Mansfield was one of the largest towns in the UK without a train service (except for a distant 'Parkway'). Due to collaboration between the Nottingham and Derbyshire county councils, the Nottingham City Council and the Strategic Rail Authority, a series of old railway lines that had been freight only for years were linked up to provide a new train service between Nottingham and Worksop, to be known as the 'Robin Hood Line'. It opened in stages between 1993 and 1998 and now carries over one million passengers per year. The new station at Mansfield is exquisite and includes this wonderful all-over roof across the up bay platform. In 2005, No 170505 is almost ready to leave for Nottingham. *Author*

▼ The financial viability of a branch line could be greatly enhanced if there was regular freight traffic, although precise costings and the amount of any income contribution were never made available at pre-closure public meetings. Hopefully adding to the coffers of the remaining Bedford to Bletchley line was this empty waste train, seen joining the old bullhead rail of the branch at Forders Sidings near Stewartby in September 1993, behind now-withdrawn Railfreight 'Grid' No 56056. The train is returning to collect another load of household waste from the Capital. *Author*

▲ Matlock was once part of the Midland Railway double-track main line from London St Pancras and Derby to Manchester Central. The line beyond Matlock and over the Peak District as far as Chinley closed to passengers in July 1968 and since that time the station seen here has been the terminus of a branch line from Derby and Ambergate. With the most wonderful backdrop dominating the scene a Central Trains two-car unit, No 156401, has just arrived from Derby and will shortly return. The old down platform has all but disappeared but the fine up side infrastructure remains, which includes a highly recommended Peak Rail shop. *Author*

▼ It was a great surprise in 1986 when the news filtered through that the reopening of part of the old Oxford to Cambridge route was imminent. The line east of Oxford had closed to passengers from January 1968, but during 1987 NSE proposed to reopen the line as far as Bicester. The station would be called Bicester Town with an intermediate station at Islip. In this March 1988 view, DMU No L205 pauses at the resuscitated station before departing for Oxford. There are exciting plans by Chiltern Railways to build a new spur from here to connect with their Banbury to Marylebone line, providing an Oxford to London via High Wycombe service. The proposed ready-for-service date is 2013. *Author*

▲ More privatisation, this time in Lancashire as First (Group) North Western-liveried Class 142 'Pacer' No 142001 poses in the rain at Blackpool South in June 2003. One interesting aspect of the privatised railway is not only the seemingly endless changes in franchisee, but the perpetual tinkering with train liveries. The driver is changing ends while the guard is in contact with the junction signalbox at Kirkham & Westam. Again, the poor old rail passenger is consigned to a glass box, albeit with a curved roof, to shelter from the elements. The train will travel through to Colne via Preston. *Author*

▼ Austerity personified at Morecambe featuring yet another cheap and unimaginative modern station comprising an island platform, clinical lamp standards and a comfort-free zone called a shelter. There can be no comparison between this abomination and the lovely old Promenade station already featured (see page 130). These trippers will not be pleased at the leaden skies as they alight from No 150133 in June 2003, into a world of Burger King and Blockbuster. Notwithstanding the destination blind the unit will shortly return to Lancaster. *Author*

▲ On arrival at Blaenau Ffestiniog from Portmadoc in July 1997, courtesy of the Ffestiniog Railway, it was both a surprise and a pleasure to be greeted by this retro-painted green-liveried DMU for the onward journey down the Conwy Valley to Llandudno Junction. No 101685 was resplendent with attention to detail, such as the red buffer beam and accurate BR bodyside transfers, being a credit to all concerned. Such units served the country for nearly 50 years and no branch line rolling stock before or since has been as popular with the travelling public. Why is it now so difficult to have observation windows at each cab end and seats that actually line up with the windows? It's hardly rocket science! *Author*

▼ A modern but attractive scene featuring the classic main line to branch interchange. The scene is Oxenholme on the West Coast Main Line and a delicate balance between old and new has been successfully achieved. The old station buildings on the right have been pleasantly integrated with today's railway, while on the left the overall roof across the Windermere branch and down main line platforms has been tastefully refurbished using modern materials. Windermere-bound Alstom 'Coradia' unit No 175113 was only three years old when photographed in June 2003. *Author*

▲ These old wooden crossing gates, still with their red enamel warning circles attached, are acting as a trellis for local foliage on the old freight spur from Totton in Hampshire down to Eling Wharf on Southampton Water. The siding once hosted ARC stone and Redland Tiles freight terminals, but that is a matter of history. In addition to the gates the old track across the adjacent road also remained when photographed in June 2004. *Author*

▼ Truly the end of the line and also the end of the illustrative content of our long journey through the 'Rise and Fall' years of British Railways. To summarise, the railway network of 1948 had to change. Hopelessly uneconomic lines and stations had to close unless they were to be perpetually and heavily subsidised by the public purse. Somewhere along the line a Beeching-style review would have been necessary. From the closures of the 1960s and the lows of the 1970s there have been some signs of railway regeneration, but even privatisation has not produced a profitable railway. This has been a nostalgic journey, which I hope you have enjoyed. These rusting buffer stops are at Pembroke Dock station and single car No 153302 pauses at the old derelict station in July 1997, appropriately the last year of British Rail train operation. *Author*

INDEX